IVALU • THE ESKIMO WIFE

AMS PRESS

NEW YORK

IVALU

THE ESKIMO WIFE

BY PETER FREUCHEN

AUTHOR OF "ESKIMO"

TRANSLATION BY JANOS JUSZTIS

AND EDWARD PRICE EHRICH

NEW YORK · LEE FURMAN, INC.

1935

Library of Congress Cataloging in Publication Data

Freuchen, Peter, 1886-1957.
  Ivalu, the Eskimo wife.

  Reprint of the 1935 ed. published by L. Furman, New York.
  I. Title.
PZ3.F895Iu7   [PT8175.F65]   839.8'1'372   74-5834
ISBN 0-404-11639-6

Reprinted from an original copy in the collections
of The University of Alaska Library.

From the edition of 1935, New York
First AMS edition published in 1975
Manufactured in the United States of America

AMS PRESS INC.
NEW YORK, N. Y. 10003

To

RUTH BRYAN OWEN

*in appreciation of
her friendship
for the Eskimos*

IVALU • THE ESKIMO WIFE

Chapter One

THE year Ivalu was born was the year of the big wood famine. The people did not have enough wood for their sleds, and the *kayaks* which they could make were miserable. It was impossible to paddle them straight, because they could not be made from large, strong pieces—only from little pieces tied together. The men said that the women were at fault because the skin coverings were badly sewn. But, after all, they could safely blame the women for anything, and whether they beat the women because of the *kayaks* or for a different reason, did not matter much. For the women knew that the men beat them not only because they lacked the necessary wood, but also because they were not able to understand and bear their poverty.

This greed for wood made the people move to Cape York on the windward side of the island, for to this place the big white men came with their ships when they travelled north for whale fishing. Nobody knew where these ships came from, but the white men were immensely rich and glad to trade. They bought fox skins and bear skins and women and narwhal teeth. So the people brought all these to Cape York, and they asked only for wood in payment.

When the ship had gone, the women would chatter among themselves and relate their experiences; the children would shout with pleasure about the things they had seen on the boats—but the men would feel their wood, looking for knots and measuring the size of the pieces with their fingers.

Then, one day, the people saw that an enormous wooden ship was drifting in to shore. They gathered down near the water and the men said to one another: "Perhaps the white men regret that they have paid us only in wood! Perhaps they would have preferred to spare other things. Now, out of scorn, they are sending us a whole ship of wood, for us to take as much as we want, and the next time ask for other goods!"

Never had there been such great happiness among them. They watched the ship drift in closer, and they wondered why no one came out to be seen. Finally, when it was very close, the people paddled out and climbed on board. They saw that the ship was filled with many treasures—and they also saw that all the white men were lying around, dead. They had no wounds—they were just dead. So the people undressed them, kept part of their clothing, and threw the bodies overboard. They were white men who could not demand protection from the spirits of the people, so they thought that the usual burial was not necessary. Right now they were not thinking of burial or customs; for the ship was filled with white men's food and with all sorts of wonderful things.

They brought many valuable things to shore, and every time two of the people met they had to stop and laugh aloud in their great happiness. They only stopped to laugh, and then hurried back to the ship and got even more of the treasures. And, after carrying things ashore for several hours, they got tired and went to sleep.

But ak! when they awoke, the ship was far out to sea! In their stupidity the people had forgotten to tie it to the coast, as the white men used to do. They had been so excited over all the things on board for which no payment was asked that they had forgotten their need for wood. They had taken scarcely any, and now they regretted having thought only of the things they wanted—not of what they needed.

But the World-Spirit would not stand for such immodest behavior, and as punishment for their greed she sent illness over the people. Some of them said that one of the white men had returned as a ghost, to help bring misfortune upon them. Because on the day after the ship drifted away, one of the corpses, which had been thrown overboard, was sighted. It had sunk at first, but now it came up again. It stood straight up in the water and stared with glaring eyes toward the land. Yes, it was undoubtedly a ghost which could not find its way to land, because it was on strange shores. So it drifted away—but not before it had wished the sickness and death on the people.

An old man named Talagatina was the first one to get sick. His thoughts were disturbed by the heat in his head, and he was very dangerous. Nobody dared go near him. But his little daughter did not know she should fear her father, and when she went to him in his madness he grabbed her and choked her to death.

A few days later he became quiet again, and they told him what he had done in the absence of his mind. "From now on," he said, "my life would be more difficult than death." The others understood, and did not stop him when he climbed to the top of the cliff and threw himself into the sea. He was offering himself to the dead to satisfy the curse which was on him.

Soon more and more people got sick. Some lost all their strength suddenly, and sank to the ground; others became mad for a while and then the same thing happened to them, too. But all those in whom the disease spread, died.

Horror took hold of the people of the settlement and they fled from Cape York. Some of them went across the island, to the big seal place, and filled the houses of the families there. But the World-Spirit was still not satisfied. She avenged herself also on those who offered hospitality to those meant for death, so that the fugitives and those who took them in were likewise caught in the net of death. That summer was full of misfortune for the people who lived on the windward side.

Some of the young men and their families had taken their *kayaks* and paddled across to an island, called Steep-Isle, in order to escape the terrible disease. Among them were Ungudluk and Kazaluk, Ivalu's mother and father, and Ivalu herself, with her younger brother.

At Cape York the people were still dying. And whenever someone died, according to the laws of the ancients, one must remain in his house for five days. One must not even go out for catch, in order not to insult the spirits. So the seals lay on the new fall ice; birds swarmed over the mountains and the white whales breathed in the ice fissures, swimming back and forth near the shores of the settlement. The children saw them and shouted that wonderful food was swimming there, but the grown-ups could do nothing. They could only wish that they were like the children, unaware of the hard laws which forbade catching during the period of death.

The summer passed. Sometimes they saw ships out at sea, but they could not get to them. The early ice pressed close to shore, too thin as yet to bear the weight of their sleds. It seemed as though the World-Spirit did not want the people to have contact with the white men who had sent them a whole ship which they shamefully had let escape.

In the settlement only two men were left alive. One was a man named Uvdluriak, who had had great sorrow forced upon him by the events of the summer. For the disease had taken his wife, too, with the wives and husbands of many of the others. It was very sad for Uvdluriak because his feeling for his wife had changed him from a reckless young man into a great catcher, and she had given him his small son.

In his youth he had travelled from settlement to settlement with other young men, laughing and amusing himself, courting the women and not courting them in vain. But he never gathered food or had clothes prepared for the winter, so, when the cold and dark did come, he had difficult times. His wife made him industrious, and filled him with the desire to have many possessions. She had taught him that it was pleasant to possess much meat, and so be able to shout to arriving strangers, "Come to my house—eat, and feed your dogs!" Often he overdid this hospitality and then was unhappy because the strangers' dogs lacked appetite. But this would happen only after he had fed them so much meat that they could not eat any more. Then everybody would laugh and say, "This hospitality of Uvdluriak's is like a legend!" And he could see how happy this praise made his little wife.

But now she was dead. He watched them place the last skin over her head before they sewed her in for burial. He saw, in his house, the beautiful fox skin coat with its cowl of seal skin, which had made her so happy in the last year when he brought home the rare black seal. Now she was sewn in nothing but a sack. He stood there in his hut and saw them carry her out. And as they piled stones over her grave, his sorrow was so great that it gave him strength to lift larger rocks than was possible for a man to lift.

That night he heard his little son, Inuiterk, crying because he had no mother. The boy was already big enough to run out to play, but in the evenings, before he fell asleep, he was accustomed to drink from his mother's breast. Now he lay on his bed, his mouth making suckling sounds and with tears running down his dirty little face. So Uvdlurtak got up, and with his knife slit his fingers. one after the other, and let his little son suck the blood from them. For many days Uvdluriak had wounds in his fingers which hindered him out catching—but every night he cut them open again, because his little son cried and had no mother to quiet him with her breast.

He was unhappy and restless. One day, after he

15

had climbed to the top of the hill and seen that the ice was now strong all the way over to Steep-Isle, he decided to harness his dogs and go out to see what had become of those who had fled there. He went to the house of the other man who remained alive, Merquzaq, the grandfather of Ivalu. He was very old and very wise, and for a long time had done all the thinking for the people, and was their leader. The fact that he came from a distant part of the land, and that he had only one eye, made him a man whose words should be respected.

When Uvdluriak told him what he wished to do, Merquzaq and his old wife, Ama, looked at him.

"One wished greatly to hear about those on Steep-Isle," Merquzaq said. "The fate of our daughter, Kazaluk, and our grandchildren fills us with anguish. I would like to cross—but I will wait and let you bring me news from there."

Ama said she would take Uvdluriak's son, Inuiterk, into her house while he was gone, so Uvdluriak drove away.

As he came close to the iceberg bars in front of the island, the ice was thinner. The dogs were frisky, wanting to jump, and he had to hold them back by shouting, "Oh, oh! Ei, ei!" He cracked his whip over their heads so that the whiplash flicked their faces and held them back. For, when the ice is very thin, one must ride very slowly so that the sled runners will not cut through. And Uvdluriak was a master driver.

When he got closer, he saw that he would have to ride around the island and then come back over the hill, on land, because close to the shore the water was not yet frozen. He was so anxious to see people that he did not mind the dangerous trip over the snow hill. He even forgot his heavy thoughts in thinking of his visit. But, when he reached the top of the hill, he was surprised at the silence. No one could be seen around the houses.

"The men are out for catch," he thought. "Ungudluk always went out for bear earlier than any of the others. They must have left a long time ago, for there are no traces of the sleds. Ak! maybe there has been ice here for some time, and we at Cape York knew nothing about it."

But no women and children came out, either. He himself could not make any noise, or shout aloud in greeting, as he had left a settlement full of dead people. So he waited, but still no one came out to greet him.

After a while he tried to attract attention. He beat one of the dogs so that his howling in the silence flared up like a light in darkness. And then a woman came out of one of the huts. She stood in front of the entrance and looked at him. Uvdluriak sat down. He could not go to her, as he had only sad happenings to relate. The woman went back into the house.

He knew her. It was Kazaluk, the wife of Ungud-luk, with whom he had played as a child. They were equals, he and she, for her husband was a great catcher.

Then a little girl came out, and Uvdluriak saw that it was Ivalu. She was only a child and did not know how to behave according to custom. She ran directly toward him, but before she reached him she stopped and began to cry. Uvdluriak tied his dogs to a rock and went slowly toward the house into which Kazaluk had disappeared. When he reached the little girl, he stopped and looked at her. She was still crying, but only a little.

"Do you live here?" he asked her.

She did not answer.

"Have you no one to play with?"

Ivalu stopped crying and looked at him. "One is alone," she said, and started to go back to the house.

Uvdluriak followed her and stopped in front of the entrance. He had an uneasy feeling when he saw two sleds, snowed in and unused, and only few foot-steps in the snow. No road led to any of the other houses—only this one was inhabited. He felt his throat tighten. Had death also followed those who had fled to Steep-Isle? For a moment he waited, and then he decided to go in. Perhaps there were only women here, afraid of a man.

"Hock! Hock! Hock!" he called into the house passage, and bent down to drive away any dogs which might rush at him.

"Ak! there are no dogs. You have come to a house with no dogs," the woman called from inside.

He did not answer, but crawled through the passage. It was almost dark inside. Only the little light coming through the gut window lighted the horror which he saw.

Kazaluk was inside, a woman who had lived in his thoughts as being very beautiful. But now she was thin and starved,—and little Ivalu, who had been sweet and had had big eyes, looked as though she were old, and had been thinking a lot. She was so thin that it made him sad.

Neither he nor Kazaluk said anything. Presently Uvdluriak had seen everything in the house, although he pretended that he was only admiring the handle of his whip.

"Herewith one comes to visit," he said quietly.

"Does one at last come visiting?" Kazaluk answered, and then she was again silent.

But they both thought they might speak of other things, for they knew each other well and both had frightful things to relate.

"Ak! one is without a tribe," Kazaluk said. "Those who lived here before have gone to the last sleep."

"I have no happiness either," Uvdluriak said. "Many have died in my settlement."

"Are they dead, too, the great ones of Cape York?" Kazaluk asked. And they both knew that among those who lived on the windward side, mourning had become stronger than laughter.

"It happens that one is without blubber," Kazaluk said. "Ak yes! my house is without food, and we are starving, I and my little daughter."

"There is a little blubber on my sled," Uvdluriak answered. "Unfortunately it is neither good nor tasty. One is like a miserable child when it comes to providing good things."

He spoke to forget his sorrow.

"As if blubber would not always taste good to one who starves!" the woman said. And her guest went out and returned with blubber and meat.

Kazaluk's face twitched. She pulled her little daughter to her, rubbing her nose against the little girl's. Then she put the blubber into the cooking lamp.

Ivalu stuck her fingers into the soft mass of fat and then licked them clean. It was as pleasant to her as sleep is to a catcher after a long, tiresome day. Uvdluriak watched her and then went out again. He saw that the *kayaks* had been unused during the summer, and that the skins had been pulled off the frames, eaten by the dogs—or the people.

He had brought plenty of meat with him on the sled and now he laid some of it on the stone scaffold outside. Kazaluk came out and saw it.

"One will try to build a fire," she said. "There has been none burning for a long time, and there are no matches. Perhaps the ships have brought some?"

Uvdluriak gave her a box. "Maybe this will turn into fire," he said, and got busy with the lacing of his sled.

Kazaluk went in and called to Ivalu, "Now we have been given fire—and you can warm your poor fingers!"

She chewed a piece of hot blubber and spat it out on some moss. It burned with little crisp crackles. Ak! she was so skillful, this Kazaluk! She arranged the moss on the edge of the lamp with her lamp stick and, when Uvdluriak came in, the house was light. He pushed in a piece of ice for her to melt, and came crawling in behind it. He had taken off his outer furs and left them outside the stone shed.

Now he sat down in his birdskin shirt, but he had pulled the cowl up over his head. Kazaluk also wore the cowl, because she was thinking of the dead. These two were people without happiness, and had no desire to laugh. Silently Kazaluk put the pot over the fire, and broke the ice into small pieces. Ivalu watched everything. It seemed new to her that ice should melt and that afterwards meat should be cooked. She could not think of anything else. She was still a child and forgot things quickly.

Uvdluriak watched Kazaluk closely as she pushed up the wick, gave the little girl some of the warm water to drink, and then put the pot of meat over the flame.

He suddenly realized that he had forgotten his own sorrow and his little boy back home. Now he desired Kazaluk, and thinking of her and of little Inuiterk again, he thought perhaps he had found a woman for his home.

"It is not impossible that one will have to wait a few days before returning to the settlement," he said. He looked away as he said it, and let the words sound indifferent.

But Kazaluk was a woman and had sensed his thoughts long before he had put them into words. Why should she fight against them? There were no other people here to see her immodesty in not resisting. A woman needs a man. With him come food and warm clothes. Before Uvdluriak came, she and her little daughter were waiting for the death which had already taken all the other people of this settlement. She was again one of life's people, and with whom should she go if not Uvdluriak? Surely luck was still following her, when one of the most capable men in the tribe wanted her! Uvdluriak was a man who was young and gentle, and a provider who would make her envied when they went visiting to foreign places.

"Will the meat be boiling soon?" Ivalu asked. But her mother quieted her with another piece of the frozen meat. She told Uvdluriak they had not eaten meat since the sun had disappeared and the winter darkness had begun. Uvdluriak was happy that her talk was friendly. His wooing had been accepted.

Water began to trickle down from the roof, and presently it dripped from the walls and other places.

"The house is in bad condition," Kazaluk said. "I am only a miserable woman and must do everything alone."

He knew, then, that the others had died shortly after they had come to the island and moved into the huts, and that there had been no fire in the house for a long time. He helped Kazaluk, and they took bunches of dried grass from the cot and dried up some of the water.

Kazaluk took off her boots. Ak! her legs were so thin and dirty: as those of starving people always are. She rubbed them with her hands, and said she was still cold. Uvdluriak told her to light the other lamp, too, as he had plenty of blubber and she should not be afraid of wasting it.

While Uvdluriak and Kazaluk were busy trying to do a few things to improve the house, Ivalu did nothing but eat. She did not know anything except that she was hungry. And finally Kazaluk said, "The meat is cooked!"

"Let us try to eat," Uvdluriak said.

The meat lay on the stone platter—huge, wonderful pieces, thick with gravy and steaming in the cold room. Kazaluk took her meat stick, piercing the pieces in the pot and putting them on the platter, too.

"Oh, I have burned myself!" Ivalu laughed. She had grabbed a large piece of the hot food in her hand.

"Wait a little—just wait," her mother said. But Ivalu held the meat on the meat stick and ate it.

"One can eat and eat, there is so much!" she cried. "I could eat more and more, and never stop!"

And a little later they drank soup, cooked more meat, and ate again. When they were through this time, they cooked still more and put it into the pot. It was to cool off, and be there for them in case they should wake up in the night and have the desire to eat again.

There was only one miserable bed fur in the house, and Uvdluriak understood that the furs from the other beds had been used to sew the dead in— or eaten by those who were starving. It was remarkable, he thought, that the little girl had been able to live through the long months of starvation. He went out to the sled and brought in sleeping things.

"Take my skins," he said, and Kazaluk spread them out on the bed. Then they sat there for a while, staring before them, and thinking.

Ivalu had fallen asleep, and her mother started to undress her. Her little body was gray and thin from starving for so long. Uvdluriak leaned over and scratched the child's back.

"We can all become fat again," he said.

The next day they left and went back to the settlement. But here they were not happy, for it was too full of terrible memories for either one of them to want to stay. Uvdluriak was disappointed. He was happy at having a new wife to look after his little son, but the sorrows of the starving people were heavy on his thoughts. Here, he knew, were only those who would be without blubber or food or lamps when the winter came, because of the summer they had endured. They would have to come to him for these things, and the only feeling they could have for him would be a humble one. For that is the only feeling that people, who have to beg, can have for those who help them.

"One has decided to travel to the north," he finally said to Kazaluk.

"So!" she said. She felt a secret happiness, for her joy in being married was often forgotten a little because from the settlement she could see across the ice to Steep-Isle, and it made her remember the sorrow and horror of that place.

Merquzaq and Ama went with them on the journey over the glacier. Merquzaq was happy. He was with his daughter, Kazaluk, his little granddaughter, Ivalu, and his new son-in-law, Uvdluriak—and they were travelling away from their suffering, toward the many people, who lived on the leeward side of the land. Ivalu rode on the sled with her grandparents and Inuiterk rode with his father and step-mother. First their way led through a valley, then turned and passed along a flat plateau on the glacier. It was not yet really winter, when snow would cover the glacier and fill in the cracks, so it was still dangerous to pass along the sides. Uvdluriak told his son about the ghosts, who lived in the cracks and fissures and pulled down travellers to suck the blood out of them. Their ghost houses, down there, were covered with snow so one could not see them, and in them the demons sat and waited. Sometimes they had to be satisfied with a dog, but they preferred human blood.

When the road was steep, up the mountain, the travelling was a little slow. Then the grown-ups would get off and walk by the sleds, but the children stayed on and rode. They laughed and did not know that some day they, too, would have to walk and let other little children sit and rest. The dogs were well fed, fat, and not broken in to trips with heavy loads. Their tongues hung out, and they panted in the crisp, cold air.

Suddenly Uvdluriak discovered something unusual far away on the glacier. It might have been a bear. But perhaps it was just a snow house, or a rock which was sticking up through the ice. However, Uvdluriak was a hunter who never missed an opportunity.

He had stopped to untangle the harness. Now he was finished and cried, "Seat yourselves on the sleds!" And cracking his whip, he called to the dogs and started his sled in motion. He jumped on, driving hard toward the unusual object.

It turned out to be a bear, a big, yellow male that had wandered down from the north to find a place where there was peace and quiet and where he could sleep. But soon it was no longer a bear—just two piles of meat, a skin that was already split open, and a large spot of blood grinning at them from the white snow. The dogs were chewing the entrails, the grown people laughed, and the children played near them shrieking with joy. A bear is, after all, only created for the pleasure of the catch, and so that his hide can be made into trousers and his meat serve as meals for everybody.

A light snow storm began. The wind blew down from the glacier, and the snow whirled low to the ground, the kind of fine snow that is called "floor sweepings".

They loaded the sleds, putting the bearskin on the bottom and the meat on top of it. It was a big bear, and they were glad to be able to take something to the people in the north. For there were few of these animals there and they knew that the people whom they were going to visit could use the skin to make new pants.

The dogs were displeased that they had to pull after the good food, but a whip is a whip and a man is a master. Uvdluriak drove them with his "Hock! Hock!", and stayed in the lead in spite of his heavy load. He was a man who always liked to show the way, even if there was only one sled following him.

The storm grew, and the wind got much stronger. Now and then Uvdluriak would get off his sled and dig his whip handle into the snow, but it was too dry for house-building, so they went on. Kazaluk covered the children with reindeer skins, which were pulled over their heads and tied down, forming a little hut in which they could keep warm. Kazaluk did not ask how much longer they would keep on in the storm. She was a woman travelling with her husband. One of them had to decide, but it was never the wife.

Uvdluriak wanted to reach Iffisek. He knew that Kajurak lived there, with his son and brother. There was only a slight friendship between them, but there, at least, was shelter from the storm, which now really was bad. Snow and wind reigned over the glacier, and the going was almost impossible. Perhaps the ice around the foot of the hill was safe, and it would be easier to get through that way. So Uvdluriak led the dogs down, and, as they slid into the valley, they left the storm behind them.

As they came up again beyond the hill, it was quiet in the fjord. One could see houses scattered as far as the cliffs, and children were running around. As they came nearer, the dogs of the settlement began to howl, announcing the approach of sleds.

But Uvdluriak did not go too near. A lot had happened where he had come from, things which could not be shouted aloud in a happy voice. So, while they were still some distance away, he jumped from his sled, struck the ground with his whip as hard as he could, to halt his dogs, then sat down and waited for the inhabitants to appear.

Kajurak came out of his house and stood near the door. By now it was so dark he could not see clearly who the travellers were, but he did not care about that, anyway. As they did not shout a greeting, he knew that they were people who were embarrassed because they brought bad news. After standing there for a while, he went back into his house and sat there with the other men of the village.

"The event has arrived that the stomach is hungry," he said, and the others understood his intentions. They took food from the pot, and ate, and talked of everyday things. To them no visitors were near the settlement.

Uvdluriak understood what was happening and was enraged. He was ashamed that his new wife could see how he was being mocked. He could not believe that he could come to a place without hearing shouts of welcome.

"Let us try to build a miserable house!" he said, and began to cut snow blocks. In a little while the house was finished, and they moved in and were comfortable.

The settlement children ran in and out of the houses and told everybody what the visitors had done. This made Kajurak and his son feel uncomfortable.

"There are, no doubt, other houses and people in the neighborhood," Kajurak said finally. "Let us go and visit."

But the visit turned into a quarrel. At times Kajurak would shout loudly, and then his son and brother would laugh. Uvdluriak and Merquzaq felt that the settlement they had left was a more pleasant place than this, even though the people there were sad and happiness had gone from their houses.

"We travelled away from death, and now all we hear is ill talk", Uvdluriak said. "You are a man without kindness in your heart and our ears wish to close themselves to your words."

"Ak yes! but no one can resist me," Kajurak shouted. "My friendly spirits follow my wishes! It was they who sent death to your settlement, as I wished them to! Yes, when people resist me, I send illness over their settlements by my spirits!"

Old Merquzaq was seized with fear. His relatives lived in the North. It was true, the inhabitants of Cape York were all dead, and he feared he would lose all his relatives, now.

"Why do you say that, Kajurak? Why do you talk of your power and your friendly spirits? I have never heard a medicine man boast!"

"Ak! you think it is boasting? I say, no—it is not! And I shall send death on further, to every settlement you intend to visit! Let the people get sick, and many of them die, so that peace shall come over our glaciers and so no man from far away shall come and kill bears which were intended to be caught by us!"

Anger had confused his thoughts. One could understand now that he was angered because Uvdluriak had killed a bear, which had been sleeping near his own home, and which he had not discovered.

"The country is big," Uvdluriak said. "If you want meat, we shall bring you part of our catch. One has often before seen to it that the weak and sick have received their share, without themselves having to help."

The others became silent at this, and no more was said. Kajurak and his companions went home, and Uvdluriak and his family went to sleep.

The next day they could see that a storm still swept the glacier, but here in the fjord it was calm and clear. Uvdluriak decided to ride out and examine the ice around the outer hills, to see if it was safe enough to continue toward the north that way. Merquzaq went with him.

As soon as they were gone, the women of the settlement came to call on Kazaluk. Women have no share in the decisions of their husbands. When they are by themselves, they forget they have masters and talk as though they alone can say things with meaning.

"Herewith one comes to visit," they said quietly, as they entered. But Kazaluk sat there with her legs crossed and did not answer them. She looked straight ahead of her, and tears rolled down her cheeks.

The women had heard from their husbands about death's big catch in Kazaluk's settlement. They sat down and said, "Ak yes! Ak yes!" and then were silent for a long time.

"Here one sees a woman with only one child,"

Kazaluk said, finally, "My little son followed his father."

Then she told them of all the things she had experienced. She sounded as though she was glad to have listeners, and as though never before had she been able to tell so many people about her misfortunes.

"My little boy grew thinner and my breast was empty of milk because I was starving. Look here—how he chewed off my nipples!" She bared her body for them to see. "See at last what happened in a place where torture was greater than human beings could endure! But it was best for the little one to die. Thus he had peace, and his father had companionship as he had so often desired. From the day my little boy was born, my husband used to look at him and say, 'My little future catch-partner,' I thought, 'Let them hunt together on the big hunting grounds,' and so I let him die.

"Then my little daughter and I cried a great deal, for she needed a playmate to help forget her hunger. Ak! she was so wise! I asked her if she wanted to die, too, but she said she wanted to live, and promised never to cry for food. She ate grass, and even rabbit droppings!"

Kazaluk told them of her other misfortunes. She told how the others had tried to run away from death, but in vain. She forgot her own sorrow in telling of all the happenings.

The women sat with her for a long time, until Kajurak's son came running into the snow hut.

"The men call that the lamps should be taken care of, and children are crying for their mothers," he said.

The women quickly left the house and hurried home. They had enough to talk about, now, and they knew a good deal of what had happened in other places that summer.

Uvdluriak and Merquzaq returned with two seals on their sleds. They had been out to the edge of the ice, where the seals come up to breathe in the open water. Uvdluriak had received a gun and cartridges from the whale catchers, and he used this while Merquzaq used his harpoon. When the seals came up, one of the men would scratch on the ice or bark like a seal, and this made them come nearer. The young ones could even be coaxed by whistling. When they were close, Uvdluriak would shoot them, and Merquzaq would drive his harpoon into the animals and drag them in.

Uvdluriak was angry. Kajurak had refused him hospitality, and even boasted that he was the cause of the death which had tortured many of the lands on the windward side. Nor was he ashamed to show envy over a miserable bear that had been killed. Such a man must be punished, Uvdluriak thought, and he called to Kajurak's son and another boy who were passing. He stopped his dogs, and untied the seals.

"Here are two miserable seals," he said. "Take them to the big Kajurak and his brothers, and tell them that I am an unskillful, miserable catcher, and I am unable to offer them more meat!"

The boys took the seals and carried them away. Merquzaq laughed very much, and it was the first laugh on his face in many, many days. As they were tieing up their dogs, they saw Kajurak come down from the hill. He passed close to their house without talking to them.

"Ak! you there!" Uvdluriak called to him. "It so happened that one caught a pair of small seals. They are in front of your house entrance, so that you should not think we want to deprive you of catches near your home!"

Kajurak stopped and looked at them with angry eyes. He tried to find an answer but words of proper force had left him.

"One was in the mountains for a certain season," he said. "It happens that in this settlement a little calling of spirits was done; just a little calling, in order to make a few helpful spirits fulfill a very modest wish." And he raised his eyebrows, pushing his lips forward and stretching his mouth wide.

Merquzaq was an old man, full of fear for the

wisdom of the spirits of the ancients whose favor he knew Kajurak had won.

"Now listen, you who speaks," he said. "Hold back your words and leave your spirits under the ground where they live! The misfortune of death must hit no more people!"

"One has made his decisions!" Kajurak said.

No more words were spoken, but, in that moment, Merquzaq again became a young man. Strength came into his arm. Once he had belonged to those who never missed, and now again he hit his mark. Kajurak jumped to one side, but the point of the spear had pierced his shoulder and stuck there. The force knocked him backward. Quickly he was on his feet again. He pulled out the weapon, and saw he had only suffered a small wound from which the blood streamed. He pressed his hand to the wound, and wanted to run home, but he considered it wrong to turn his back on his enemies. He tried to use words to escape a second attack, which he would not have been able to resist.

"Ak! you who think you could kill me with a dull spear!" he shouted, trying to be mocking. "I shall call on my spirits! I shall call on my power! Hei-ja-hei. . . ." and he began his songs and was terrible in his words.

He hurled terrible threats. He took his hand from the wound, bloody and dripping, and pounded it like a drum hammer against his other fist. He looked frightening in the light of the sunset, which had come over them.

But Uvdluriak had his gun, and he was a man whose duty it was to see that misfortune's journey was stopped. He raised his weapon to his shoulder and shot. Kajurak croumpled to the ground—not forward and not backward, but straight to the ground as though every bone in his body had lost its hold. Then he managed to get to his feet.

"You have hit me, Uvdluriak! Yes, you have hit me in the heart, and I have been sufficiently hit! A-ja-ja-hei!"

He plunged to the ground again, in the madness and fury of the death struggle.

"My heart brought me death—and so shall your heart become your wounding point! Heia hei!"

As the people of the settlement came running, he could only move his arms and legs a little. But, when they lifted him up, his head fell over on one side, and no breath came from his mouth.

Uvdluriak and Merquzaq stood near their sleds and watched the others. All the people of the settlement had come out. Kajurak's brothers carried the dead man to their home, and talked to one another for a long while.

Uvdluriak kept watch until late that night, for

it was not impossible that they might be attacked. But finally sleep came into his head.

"A man has been killed," he said to Kazaluk, "but we who are alive wish to sleep when we need to." Shortly afterwards, he fell asleep, and no one disturbed his house during the night.

When they woke up, they saw that the settlers were burying the big catcher in the hills. The children looked on, and Inuiterk, who was already big and had seen many burials, told the other youngsters what was going to happen. They saw that Kajurak's brothers were exchanging dogs with those of the dead man, whose animals, according to custom, had to be killed. His brothers brought bad, ill-fed creatures and took his good ones. Then he was borne to the grave by a team, which had not even been broken in.

When the mourners and the body arrived at the grave, a fearful howling began. Some of the dogs could be killed immediately, but some of the others jumped around, trying to escape the blows of the axe. All the possessions of the dead man were piled near the grave; his *kayak*, his sled and all his hunting equipment.

It was a big catcher who had died, and visitors should see that the dead man had been respected according to the customs of the land.

Chapter Two

FINALLY Uvdluriak and Merquzaq could see that up on the glacier the storm no longer raged, and Uvdluriak decided that it was time for them to continue their journey.

They loaded their sleds and started further to the north. The people of Iffisek stayed in their houses, not looking at them as the men cracked their whips and the sleds began to move. They went only short distances daily, as the weather was not always pleasant. But there was plenty of catch on the way, and every day the men were able to bring home meat for Ama and Kazaluk to cook.

When they reached the settlement of Papitok, Uvdluriak decided that they had travelled long enough, and were far enough north for a little while. The memory of Cape York was going out of their minds. In fact, Ivalu and Inuiterk could hardly remember the terrible things which had happened. Children are interested only in play and listening to stories. When they can get enough to eat, too, then they have no memory for the things which grown-ups can still feel sadness about.

Here, at Papitok, they lived in a big cave, which was really an enormous house carved in the cliff. There was a very small hole through which to crawl, and a long passage, at the end of which was a big space with plank beds and many large stones under which meat could be pressed. Sidewards from the passage was another space and in here, the grown people told the children, lived a terrible ghost. They couldn't see him, but they could hear him knocking on the stones. Inuiterk told Ivalu that this spirit, Tornarzsuk, could pass through earth and stone as it did through air. He did not breathe air, like people, but sniffed up stones and snow through his nose.

The two children would stand inside, hand in hand, and listen to him knock against the stone wall. When it seemed to them that he came nearer, they would scream and run to the older people. But, in a little while, they would sneak back again, because they found their terror fascinating, and like a game. And when they would get tired of playing with this spirit, Ama would tell them stories about other wonderful things. She told them about strange animals and goblins, and when she told these stories, her voice would sound like those of the terrible creatures, and her face would show what they looked like. Ivalu would have to take hold of her grandmother's hand very hard, in order to feel that Ama was only her grandmother, or else she would have been afraid.

One day Uvdluriak was standing near the cave entrance, cleaning his gun. He must have forgotten to take out the cartridges, because suddenly there was a report and someone jumped and said, "Ak!

how that frightened me!" They all laughed a great
deal and Uvdluriak said, "My gun is like a human.
It has a soul and intentions, and wanted to frighten
someone. That is why it made me forget to take out
the cartridges."

When he said this, Ivalu ran to him, and wanted
to look at the gun, but Uvdluriak said, "Continue
playing, Ivalu, or go out to eat. On the stone outside
there are frozen brains." So she ran out there and
ate. It made her stomach cold and she got sleepy,
as usual. She ran in to the plank bed, but when she
lay down, she was no longer sleepy and wanted to
play.

"Where is Inuiterk?" she asked.

"Yes," Kazaluk said, "where is he?" She called his
name, but there was no answer.

"He must have gone outside," Merquzaq said,
and continued talking about a bear they had seen on
the ice that day. He had gotten away from them,
over on thin ice where they could not follow him, and
Uvdluriak had laughed at Merquzaq's face when the
old man had to turn back.

"Tell Inuiterk to come and drink some soup," Kazaluk said. "It is better that the children should sleep
now, so that tomorrow, when we continue our trip,
they will make up with us and not want to sleep
late."

Uvdluriak went out and called his son, but he

did not answer. The father became a little alarmed; perhaps the boy had climbed further up the mountain to look at something he had discovered. Uvdluriak went further from the entrance and called "Little catch partner! Little catch partner!" but still the boy did not answer him. After a little while he went back to the cave. "Hasn't he returned? Children are not sensible. They go far away, and then their lack of forethought brings fear to their parents."

After they had waited for some time, it seemed strange to them that Inuiterk did not come in to eat.

"Was he not playing with you in the room of Tornarzsuk?" Uvdluriak asked Ivalu, and she said yes—she hadn't thought of it before. "Ak! he has hidden himself there!" she cried.

She and her mother and grandmother went into the cave, and there they found Inuiterk—dead. The bullet from Uvdluriak's gun had pierced him right through the heart. He had not been able to cry out, not a sound had come from him, and it had been impossible for them to see him in the blackness. Now he lay there, with his eyes closed. It was clear to Kazaluk that this was what Kajurak had meant by his curse on Uvdluriak. "Your heart shall be your wounding point!" he had said. The gun had a soul and intentions, and Kajurak's helpful spirits had directed it against his murderer's own son.

Kazaluk and her mother could still hear Uvdluriak calling in front of the entrance, but they did not go out. They seemed as if turned to stone, and each time Ivalu asked her mother what had happened she said, "Keep quiet! One of our companions sleeps, and one has no playmate any more. Now it is not permitted to speak for some time, among us."

Ivalu was not allowed to go out but, before she fell asleep, she still could hear Uvdluriak, further in the distance, calling for his son. When she awoke, Uvdluriak had returned, and his face was peculiar. His eyes were angry but his voice was not hard, as when he scolded his dogs. Ama and Kazaluk showed him where Inuiterk was sleeping. And when Ivalu asked her mother if he wouldn't be cold, sleeping there without a lamp, she was again told to be quiet.

"One does not wish to hear such talk. The dead must be mourned for a little while, but one keeps silent. One must not moan for them, because this brings them a burden on their long wandering."

Later, when they were preparing to continue their journey, Ivalu said that it was sad to be without a playmate. She said this to Uvdluriak, who stopped still at her words, although he was just harnessing a dog. The dog ran off, but he stared into the air and did not move a hand.

"Ak, yes!" he said. "It is hard to miss a playmate, but it is also hard to miss a catch partner."

Kazaluk heard this, and stepped up to him and

said, "You who stand there, you must not spend time in thinking. As long as we both live there is a possibility of more children."

Uvdluriak laughed then, for the first time, but right afterwards he thought again, and shook his head and looked sad.

Then Merquzaq came to him and said, "Over on the leeward side, at Etah, I have a brother whose face I have not seen for many winters, and I have also other relatives there. So perhaps Ama and I will not turn our sleds and travel with you and your family to Umanak. We are North now, and I have decided not to return to the South without stopping first at Etah."

So he and Ama loaded their sled, and went on to Etah, while Uvdluriak decided to spend a few more days in Papitok. But, from the day of Inuiterk's death he was very quiet, and often used strong words. One day, while Ivalu was standing before Kazaluk and having her hair combed, Uvdluriak came in, and his face was very sad. He told Kazaluk that the sight of Ivalu filled him with unhappiness, for it gave him great pain to see Kazaluk with her daughter—because he had killed his own son when the word of a dead man proved itself strong. They decided, therefore, to send Ivalu to her grandparents in Etah. A sled was leaving from Papitok, and Uvdluriak and

Kazaluk arranged with the people who were travelling to take Ivalu with them.

The man's name was Ullulik and his wife's name was Kullabak. She was big and fat and unfriendly, and she rode on the sled with Ivalu and her son, a boy named Orfik. He was much bigger than Ivalu, and he always pushed her out of the fur skin under which they were sitting, so that she froze. And at night no one cared whether she was scared, so she cried very much.

Kullabak said it was stupid and unpleasant to have her as a travelling companion, so she cried even more and said she wanted to go home to her mother. She did not want to go and live with her grandmother, and she did not want to sleep with Orfik at night, because he pulled the whole sleeping skin over himself.

When she finally arrived at her grandfather's, it seemed very good to her. She never had to cry, because to her grandparents her happiness was a necessity.

Her grandfather, Merquzaq, had experienced many peculiar things. He came from far, far away, on the other side of the big sea, and on the way to this land cannibals had pushed out his eye. Once, he told her, they had been so starved that those who had died were eaten by the others. But Ivalu no longer liked to hear these stories. It was more delightful to listen to Ama's stories, about the bear and the girl; about the woman who took a worm as a foster child; and all the other stories. Most of all, she liked playing outside. Orfik lived in the settlement, too, but he couldn't play well. He was bigger than the others, and so fat that the skin which they used as a sled would not slide down the hill when he sat on it.

The time came when it got colder, and was dark a great deal. The settlers here at Etah did not possess much meat, as the summer catch had been very small because of stormy weather. It was understood that the World-Spirit felt ashamed at the many deaths at Cape York, and was showing herself as being different from what she really was.

So it was necessary for every one to be saving of food. The dogs got very little to eat, and the people felt that there were too many in the settlement for the amount of food they had. They decided to celebrate the Festival of Darkness, and then travel south to good hunting grounds. Why, they asked, should they remain here, when in one day they could get to meat pots which were never empty?

For the Festival of Darkness, they all gathered in Merquzaq's house, which was the largest and the best. The children were told to climb up on the stone beds and remain seated there until the lamps were lighted again. Then the lamps were turned down, and they were turned down in the other houses, too. As darkness filled the whole house, the children could hear that the men and women were laughing a great deal and were fighting laughing. Then they heard them fighting on the beds, and the children were frightened and held tightly to each other. Shortly Merquzaq called out, "It is well time to create light!" and the children could hear him take out his tinder box and turn the wood. Immediately a small piece of moss caught fire, and one of the women blew on it. A small blubber torch was lighted and a flame burned again on the rim of the lamp.

"It is necessary to begin the year with a new light," Merquzaq said.

The women all began to laugh, and started to dress, for everyone was completely naked.

Merquzaq brought in some little auks which had been potted in blubber, and a piece of frozen meat for the children. But ak! it was so small that the children told their fathers they wanted regular pieces. They wanted big lumps with blubber on it, but an old woman said they had only a small amount stored away on the settlement. She said the children must learn contentment, so that, when they grew up, they would not feel tortured when want reigned. At this the children felt very embarrassed and said no more, but ate their little pieces quietly. Then they all went back to their houses, and Ivalu went to sleep and knew no more of that day.

The day after, a few of the families left. It was very good that they did, for some of them had no meat left at all, and had been visiting other houses and eating at their hosts'. One was ashamed when one could not offer them anything, but afterwards the others said it was immodest of them to come visiting when they knew that each house had only few provisions.

All the sleds were prepared for the journey, for no one wanted to remain in the settlement. Merquzaq, however, did not want to leave without any provisions for the trip, even if it was only a day's journey. He decided to take advantage of the moonlight and go to the breathing holes of the seals and see if there was not a possibility of catch. But, by the time he returned home, all the others had left. They would not wait for him, even though Ama told them it was sad to be left alone.

When his sled returned to the house, Ivalu went out with her grandmother to meet him, and they saw at once that he brought no prey. But it was good he had returned, for a violent snowstorm had started. It was so violent that it would have been foolish to try and start out after the others.

"How good that you have come," Ama said. "We are all alone in the settlement. The others have gone."

"One rode out to try the swiftness of the dogs," Merquzaq said. "Unfortunately there are ice fissures all over, and the breathing holes are hidden beneath the uneven surface."

So they went into the house, and sat with only one little blubber flame, in only one lamp.

"The event has arrived that today there will be no eating," Merquzaq said. But Ama pushed a little bite over to Ivalu, who stuffed it into her mouth and immediately swallowed it.

"More," she said. "I haven't had enough."

The old couple laughed and handed her a piece of meat. They knew well that it was all they had, but it made them happy not to keep it for themselves. Ivalu ate that, too.

After she had slept for a long time, she called her grandmother and said she wanted to get up. Her Ama answered her in the darkness and said she should sleep a lot more. She lay down and a long time passed until she spoke again. Her grandmother told her that now it was storming, and it was impossible to get meat. Ivalu began to cry and said she didn't care if it stormed. She only wanted something to eat, and she wanted to go back to her mother and not remain with grandparents who did not even have anything to eat. At this the old people did not answer her; it was dark in there and she could not see their faces.

Ama started to tell her stories. She told about the

little girl who came to the bear, but Ivalu interrupted her. No, she did not want to hear anything, she wanted to eat. Then Ama told about the man who once paddled out for catch and met the little midgets who lived on the shore. Here Ivalu began to shout for Ama to be quiet, and said she did not want her for a grandmother any more. The story about the woman who took the worm for a foster child only made her cry more—but then the grandmother told about Arazang. He was a man, who changed himself into all sorts of animals, and through that gathered wisdom for human beings. This was such an amusing story, and had so many peculiar sounds of animals, that the little girl forgot her hunger, and in a short while fell asleep again.

When she awoke, the storm had stopped a little, and Merquzaq was going out to see if he could not catch a hare which might have hidden behind a rock. He told Ivalu that it was necessary that no one should cry in the house, because hares have long ears and can hear when children are complaining and impatient.

So Ivalu stayed quiet in the dark, and either lay on the warm body of her grandmother, or played with her dolls. Ama had taught her to feel them when they could not be seen. They were carved from walrus teeth, and the game she played with them was so amusing she did not cry any more.

Then, from afar, Ama heard her husband calling to her that he was bringing home something to eat. "Ak!" the old woman cried, "has catch come to the house? Now catch has come to the house!"

Ama ran out to receive him. Shortly they both returned and told the child that two hares had been caught, because they had hidden from the storm without wanting to hear whether enemies approached.

They lit a very small fire, heated water, and cooked a little meat. They ate until Ivalu had enough, and she did not care that the older people ate very little. After all, they were her grandparents, and always did what they wanted.

"Are you not happy," she said to her grandfather, "that I stopped crying and so got you two lovely hares?"

"Ak yes! you can believe that I am," Merquzaq said, "and I want to thank you for helping me so well."

Both old people laughed, and Ivalu thought it must be because they were happy and grateful for her help.

Now many days passed—many, many days. Sometimes they killed a dog, and then Ama would lie in the passageway and burn wood to cook the meal, as their blubber was all used up. In the end they had only five dogs left, but it was impossible to travel in such weather. Then, finally, Merquzaq came in one day and said that the World-Spirit had no more power to resist the people's desires. The clouds had opened a little and good weather wanted to come out again.

"One tries to hold a look-out," he said, and went out. He remained away a long time, but when he returned he brought only one little auk, which he had found as he followed the track of a fox to his lair. They cooked the bird in water, but only drank the soup. On that day they got no more to eat.

On the following day they were to leave. All three were freezing, but Ivalu was packed into fur covers, her face turned away from the wind. Both Merquzaq and Ama walked by the sled, for the dogs were starved and had no strength to pull.

They rode south from Etah, and when they came to the big foothills in front of the glacier, they stopped to let the dogs rest. Then they cooked the same little auk again, and divided it among themselves.

It was slow going on the glacier. The little girl was warm and comfortable in her furs. She saw her grandmother walking ahead, while Merquzaq was holding on to the sled rod and was using his whip so much that the dogs howled.

Suddenly they saw the dogs point their ears and lift their heads. Immediately the zeal for catch caught

Merquzaq. He threw himself on the sled and drove hard. . . .

And then they were right in it.

Snow houses were standing there; sled rods were sticking up out of the snow; and they saw all the dead people. Dogs had dug up and partly eaten many of them before they themselves had been eaten by the last to die.

Merquzaq looked around and found the dead body of his brother, who had left with the others from the settlement.

Suddenly they heard a voice from inside one of the half-buried houses, and when they cut a hole in the snow wall, they saw that a woman was lying there. It was Kullabak—the strong, invincible Kullabak and her son, Orfik. All the others were dead; thirteen men had started on their long sleep here on the glacier because the snowstorm had stopped them from continuing their journey. They all died, the big people. Only Kullabak and Orfik were left, but without the strength to flee from this place where death had made its catch with starvation. Ama thought how wise Merquzaq had been in his decision not to start without provisions!

"Take my boy on your sled," Kullabak said. "I myself am unable to walk, but he shall live and learn to avoid that which he has seen here! Death has already planted his teeth in my legs!"

Ak! Orfik looked miserable. Ivalu remembered that he used to be fat, but now he was thin and ugly, and she began to cry because he was going to travel with them. She was scared of a companion who did not smile when he looked at her. But Merquzaq explained that he was a human being who wished to flee from death. "As we all have the same fear in our bodies, we must help those who need assistance!"

So Orfik was put on the sled. His mother did not say parting words to him—she only asked them to seal the house again when they left, so that she could have a pleasant death. . . .

When they finally reached the ice, it was slow going. Now and then Orfik got off the sled and helped to push it. When they finally arrived at a place where a house stood, Merquzaq stopped, opened it, and let them in. As soon as the skins had been spread over the bed planks, the old man said that he and his wife were going out on the ice to see if there was catch. Meanwhile, Orfik was to watch over the little girl so that she should not cry.

The boy had a knife in his pocket, one of those fine knives that are clapped together and can hide the blade in themselves. In the darkness, Orfik took out his knife and let her touch it. Then he put his nail in a small furrow and opened it so she could notice how sharp it was. Then she fell asleep.

The boy cut himself on the foot. In some places it

hurt and in others he did not feel it at all. He knew well that his foot was frozen, and in trying to see how far he could cut in before it hurt, he completely cut off his small toe. But it did not seem like anything more than carving a piece of wood. At this, he was so surprised that he woke up Ivalu.

"Look!" he said, "I have cut off my toe without noticing it!"

This impressed Ivalu, and she played for a while with the knife—and the toe. But then she got tired of playing and said, "My grandfather has only one eye, because he cut out his other eye, once, when he needed something to play with!"

She didn't want to say such words. They had just come into her mind while she played. Orfik listened attentively and felt he was an insignificant man, because he had only a toe to show against an eye.

Then they sat together for a long time and talked about how, when the world was light again, they would go out for catch together and eat wonderful things. Ivalu said she could eat a whole reindeer herself, without stopping, but this Orfik would not believe. He said he was too big to believe it, and that made Ivalu cry. She said that she, too, would be big some day—her grandmother had told her so—and then she could eat anything. Orfik began to quiet her:

"Listen—one must take care of you so that you

shouldn't cry!" Then he dried her eyes and they remained sitting quietly for some time.

Suddenly they heard the dogs outside begin to yelp.

"What's this?" Orfik said. "Did you hear? Maybe catch is coming here!"

Then they heard somebody shout from the ice— "Nau! Nau! We caught a walrus! We caught a walrus"

It was far away and they were sitting in a house, but their ears were so glad to hear these words that the sound penetrated to them.

"That is grandfather!" Ivalu cried—and Orfik said no more about his weakness. He forgot that many men who had suffered the same starvation as he had, had died. He almost got strength enough to run, and he went out, untied the dogs, and drove them in the direction of the sound.

"Ahau! Ahau!" Merquzaq was calling, and often had the dogs listened to that call and gotten food for it. Now, although they had almost lost the habit of eating, they rushed toward him to get their reward.

He had caught a walrus, and as the dogs arrived he harnessed them to the animal. He pulled with them and Ama pulled with them, and together they brought the walrus partly up on the ice. It was new ice and bent under the weight of the heavy animal, so that the water reached over Merquzaq's feet, but still he stood there and cut out great lumps of meat. He ate little, but Ama filled her mouth and threw warm pieces to the dogs, who swallowed them with wild greed. Then they pulled the walrus up further and cut off more meat. After they had a lot, and were so tired they could hardly move, Merquzaq let his catch slide back into the sea. He had gotten enough to save himself and his family.

They came home with the meat and lighted Ama's lamp.

"People are so peculiar," the old woman said. "For now one is not tired any more. Now we shall cook and drink soup."

She put blubber into the brew and they ate and drank their fill. Before they fel lasleep they filled the lamps with fresh blubber. And, although the house had been deserted all winter, it began to get warm, and shortly the little family that had escaped starvation was asleep.

But Orfik still thought of his mother. The following morning he decided to go after her, but Merquzaq and Ama were too weak to help him.

"My dogs are bad," Merquzaq said, "and one needs to sleep more."

Orfik did not give up. He took meat on his back and took the long road back to where his mother was all alone with the dead. When she heard him coming, she began to sing. He opened the house and called in to her, "The event has arrived that one brings a little meat."

"Ak! it is my son who comes," Kullabak said. "It seemed to be a ghost. Many assisting spirits came near to us, and I have sung for all of them to continue to help you. And now you have returned! Happiness over the sight of you!"

"Yes, happiness in great measure," Orfik answered. "The road here was far."

"Ak! was it far?" said his mother. "Ak! why did you return?"

Then it showed itself that Kullabak could not walk.

"One has to be left behind," she said. "It is necessary for your own safety." But, by that time, Orfik had already taken a snow knife from the many implements lying among the houses, cut free a sled from the snowdrift, and cleaned it.

"Seat yourself on the sled," he said. "One will try to push."

He had also found himself a harpoon, a lance, and a clasp knife with a beautiful handle. He took these, and pushed the sled first down the glacier and then over the ice. It went slowly and was difficult for him. He lost his thoughts; it pained him so in his body that he did not feel it any more. He became a dog who was only using his legs; he became a ship that was sailing by itself, without any feeling. But he finally succeeded in getting his mother to the place where the others were. There Kullabak remained seated on the ice.

"Fortunate it was so dark," she said. "If light had been over the land, so that one could see how far it was, this ride would never have happened."

Now the others came out and called a welcome, and Kullabak crawled into the house.

"Herewith one comes to visit," she said, in order to be casual in her speech and not to remind them of the dead, which she had left behind.

"Does it happen that you are on a journey?" the others asked, also trying to be casual.

But, while they were cooking meat, the strong woman began to cry. "Ak! one has gotten weak," she said. "I cry like a little child, although there is no pain in my body."

The others sat quietly and did not speak. They looked down in front of them, and noticed only the stones. So they sat a long while, until it began to bubble in the pot.

"A little meat is cooked," Ama said.

And they all ate and afterwards drank the broth. The pot was filled again and put on the fire, the blubber lamps gave heat, and the inhabitants of the house found a sleep that lasted long.

Chapter Three

IT is the sun which brings life to the people. When, in the spring, she begins to climb over the top of the mountain, she makes it seem as though this land and ice were not really the same land and ice in which one has lived in darkness for so long. It takes light to reveal it as it actually is.

People are not satisfied with the same thing for any length of time. They are happy when the sun wants to go away in the fall, and the ice binds the waves so that one can travel and visit strange settlements. But, when darkness is over them, they realize that this happiness was a mistake. The children long to look out over the land again; the men are reminded that good catching in the darkness is only an accident; and the old women gather shadows and black air, shut them into sacks and boxes, and conjure them away, to try to make the world light again.

The old Semigak always drove the darkness into the mountain caverns and crevices, and that hurried the return voyage of the sun. And now, once again, she was lighting up the top of the mountain.

The children ran around and played when they discovered it was really she directly across the settlement on the foothills; (here at Neqe one can look far out to sea), and they also saw that she was shining over the Crooked Knife Mountain out on the island.

They all ran to the houses and called to the people inside through the windows:

"Look, look, the sun wants to crawl up, the sun wants to leave her house! Do come out and look; don't sit in your houses and think that it is dark out here where we play!"

All the old people came out. They spoke words which were wise but which the children did not understand. When people have lived very long, then they talk about things that happen, but the very young, those who like to play, don't care to listen because there is nothing pleasant in the talk of old people. Their talk is too often about something that one must or must not do.

The next day one could see a piece of the sun plate even on the rim of the sea (there where the sky collides with the ice in the far, far distance, where only the clever dog-drivers can get to). The children gathered and called: "The sun is coming out of her house passage and is on her way to the sky!"

Orfik said that the sun was running up there, running for fear from her brother, the moon, who was after her. Then the old people came out of their houses, and said that everybody should take off their mittens and push aside the cowls from their heads, stretch their arms into the air, and show the sun their hands and their hair. Then she would send health over the land and those who did this would not die before the sun returned the next year, because she would know them all and would want to see their faces again.

So they all took off their mittens. Even the hands of the smallest children, who were sitting in the knapsacks, were taken out. It became cold for the children's fingers and noses because the wind was sharp. They began to say that this wasn't amusing, and that they'd rather run and continue playing. But the grown-ups answered that afterwards they could go in and eat delicacies, like aged walrus liver, but that was only for those children who resisted the cold.

Little Tafingoaq began to cry and said that her fingers were too cold and she did not wish to see the sun.

"The sun can stay away! We can still play. And if I don't get walrus liver, then I'll simply cry, and my father will give it to me anyway!"

At this all the grown-ups laughed, and Tafingoaq's mother put her mittens and cowl back on her. Ama, however, stepped immediately to Ivalu and said to her that there was danger for Tafingoaq, and for any other little girl without strength in her will who thought it was sufficient if she cried for what she wanted. In this way Ama awoke pride in the other children. Now they were not afraid to freeze a little.

But the sun crawled down again. It must have

been too cold for her to stay out long on the first day. But one could see that the mountains were happy over the return of the sun, for they were red a long time after she had gone back into her house.

The next day she came back again, and this time her whole body was in the sky, but still she did not stay long. Orfik said that the sun only wanted to see whether the new ice was strong enough to hold her in the sky, and when she found it was only strong enough close to shore, she had to go back again quickly. The third day the children were so accustomed to seeing her that they did not talk about the sun any more. It seemed to them that someone was sitting in the sky who was always there. It seemed good that when they wanted to sleep, she went away, and that when they wanted to get up to play again, it would surely be light.

One day they got the idea of trying to run so fast that their shadows would be left behind them. Orfik laughed at them and said one must jump, or else one must have as many dogs as existed in the whole settlement to pull one's sled. Then they tried to jump away from their shadows, and, when they did this and looked sidewards, it seemed as though it was difficult for the shadows to follow them. The shadows seemed to be bending a little backwards in the jumps because they had to hurry so to follow their masters. Orfik laughed again, and said that that was only because the shadows were running next to them over pieces of uneven ice.

The sun crawled always higher in the sky and now it was so light that their eyes began to hurt them.

Merquzaq decided to travel to the far north to shoot bears and several sleds followed him. They rode to the north of Etah, but instead of going the short way, in a straight line, they rode around in back of the glacier. Nobody said why they did this, but they all knew that this way they would not pass the place where the people had died in the winter. Nobody had been there to bury them; they lay on the glacier and were destined to drop into the water, when the icebergs broke off from the glacier and began to float away from the shore.

Merquzaq and his companions travelled far to the north. As often as they saw bears, Merquzaq was left behind. His dogs were not fast enough to race with the others. One could see that they had starved all winter and had not yet gotten their strength back. He who is thin but has a bloated belly must not think he is fat and full of strength.

But they rode on. At times the catch was so meagre that the dogs got no food for a few days. Then again, when a bear was killed, the dogs ate, and slowly the difference between Merquzaq's dogs and the others disappeared.

One day Merquzaq was the closest in pursuit of a bear. He passed the other sleds and reached the bear while the others were still far away. At this he laughed very much and became desirous of getting even with them for their mockery. So he let his dogs go, took hold of his spear, and faced the bear. The bear had jumped on a little ice-knoll which the dogs could not climb. Here he remained standing and watched the other hunters come riding eagerly on their sleds. One dog after another was let loose and came panting, jumping at the bear. Merquzaq himself remained motionless and looked at his hunting companions. They all took their spears and ran forward, but one who had a gun sat down at a little distance, shot at the bear, and hit him. The bear sank on its knees and all the others rushed up and plunged their spears into the animal's body. The bear fell down and the dogs hurled themselves on him so that the men had trouble driving them away. When the dogs had been beaten off, they all ran around in circles in their excitement.

Merquzaq stopped and laughed. The others were surprised that he had not used his spear at all, and that he had not taken advantage of his luck in being the first to reach the bear.

"Ak! one forgot to catch," he said. "It was so amusing to see your faces. You surely are great hunters, but I have decided to travel a little more to the north. It has proved impossible for me to get meat as long as I am in the company of such capable people."

Merquzaq called his dogs together, harnessed them, and drove toward the north. He did this to show a beginning of animosity, and the others felt ashamed that they had been so immodest. They felt that they could not look one another in the face. They only skinned their bear and divided the meat in silence.

It was around the time when they were to sleep so they did not go on, but built a snow house and went to rest. During the night came a snowstorm and by morning the tracks of Merquzaq had disappeared. "Let the peevishness of an old man alone," said a young man. "Now one has caught enough and the home journey stands ahead."

The others began to laugh and said it was too bad that the young man was always lonesome for his wife.

"Ak, let us return quickly so that he will be satisfied, and can see that no one robs him of his husbandly pleasures." At this they all laughed again, and as the weather got better, they rode home.

When the people of the settlement saw the sleds arrive they all ran out to receive the homecomers, and Ama and Ivalu saw immediately that he of whom they thought was not among them.

"Is grandfather dead?" asked Ivalu. But Ama seized her by the shoulder, shook her a little and said she must not speak like that.

"One does not see your grandfather but as long as one was greeted with much noise and happy shouts no one is dead. At such talk the World-Spirit can easily feel hurt, and she might think it best to do that which was spoken without thought."

Meanwhile, Merquzaq rode to the north. He rode far, further up than men had ever been, and he did not think of turning back. He rode till the sea became narrower and he could see the stones on both shores. And, as the dogs scented something in the west, he rode across, and there he found big things.

At first he saw a great deal of wood lying on the shore and later he found houses big as icebergs. There were two houses but there were no people, and suddenly he realized that this was the place of which he had heard. Here, at one time, white men had lived, the same white men who could not exercise their will to leave the country because a ship did not come to get them.

They had, as they moved to the south, carried a boat, but as they lacked food they had finally·lain down to die across from Etah. Later, when most of them were dead, a ship had come.

One seldom laughs when one is alone, but Merquzaq laughed as he thought of his comrades. Now he stood in the midst of the desires of many men. There was much more than a sled could carry. Here stood boxes with all sorts of meat; here was tea, and sugar (which he recognized from ships he had been on), and he thought of how happy little Ivalu would be when she got some of these good things. He decided to come here next spring with his family and a few friends from the settlement, for here were big treasures which did not have to be killed.

When he again arrived home at the settlement, it was spring. The rivers were beginning to flow and the seals were lying on the ice sunning themselves. The people sat outside in the calm weather and warmed themselves, and over the blubber fires around the settlement meat was cooking.

Many strangers from the south had come to Neqe to catch walruses, and, although there were many onlookers, Merquzaq drove by the ice fissures in the shallows so quietly that he was seen only after he was quite near. On this day he had travelled far, so he had fed his dogs well in the morning and now they did not yelp with joy or show the least desire to hurry. Silently he drove up on the land toward his house. The snow had begun to melt and his dogs lay down on a bare patch to rest, and fell asleep right away.

Merquzaq remained seated on his sled and the people did not recognize him right away, but Ama, who was anxiously awaiting his arrival, knew the dogs and went to meet her husband.

"Herewith one returns," he said, only.

"Joy, joy! The greatest joy to see you," Ama said, and Merquzaq got up to tie his dogs.

"Help me with my dogs," he said to the woman. From this she saw that he had big news to tell, for he came so quietly and with no excitement.

By now all the people of the settlement came running and shouted that they were happy to see the great trapper return.

"Ak! at last the one who does not shun long journeys is home! We have waited a long time for you," they shouted. No one asked directly, but they, too, felt that he had things to relate which would surprise them.

Merquzaq paid no attention. He tied his dogs and complained only that one of his female dogs had a bad habit of rubbing off its harness.

"Have you been far away?" they asked.

They saw that he had many boxes on the sled, objects of wood which always contain the white people's goods.

The big boxes were piled over musk-deer skins, bear skins and much meat. It was an enormous load, and underneath the sledskins lay long boards and wooden poles for harpoons and *kayak* building.

"Did you finally return home?" they kept repeating. "Ak! one has been lonesome to see the great Merquzaq." But Merquzaq seated himself on the sled and busied himself with his boots.

"Did you experience unusual things? Where have you been? What has happened?"

They were all curious and forgot to show the children that one must not crowd a newly arrived with questions, but must let people themselves tell what they want.

"Ak, yes!" said Merquzaq. "It happened that one travelled far and had a few experiences."

"What did you see? Surely you have been on the other side of the sea, as you have musk-ox skins. Have you caught musk-oxen? Did things happen which one would wish to hear?"

"Ak! I am sorry for you," said Merquzaq. "It is too bad that you have lived here and have found nothing to interest you, and that you must be satisfied with hearing about what a poor traveller has accidentally found."

"What is it, then? What is it, then?" They all spoke at once. "Tell us! One wishes to hear!"

"Ak! my boots wore through last night," said Merquzaq. "So one was forced to return home early. There is nothing else I can tell you after that difficult journey."

"Ak! the great Merquzaq," they said and laughed among themselves. For here was a man who was thoroughly accustomed to travel far, as he had been born in a distant part of the land.

"What sort of wood is this?" they asked now, directly, and began to feel it and to pull at it to see whether they were long or only short pieces.

"Well, yes," said Merquzaq, "one took a few miserable pieces of wood from the houses one found on the way."

Now the others became silent. This Merquzaq! Did he not leave the others with mocking words? And now he found wooden houses on his way! Perhaps he had been to the country of the white people on his journey, perhaps he had encountered ships; and those who stood farthest behind in the line began to say to each other that they would be wise to follow a man who was never too old to be still more capable than the others.

Merquzaq was not interested in questions and answered their talk unwillingly and sparingly. But now they stopped talking, because Merquzaq had opened the lacing of the sled and they could see boards and long poles. Two axes and two saws were lying under his sled skin, and, after he had thrown off the wood, he rolled off large quantities of meat and skins. After that, he reached into a box and pulled out something peculiar, which he handed to Ivalu, turning away from her as he did so.

"One brought away something unimportant," he said.

It was packed in the thin skins on which white men mark down their thoughts in fine lines. Ama took it away from her and unpacked it.

"No! No!" Ivalu cried. "Let me! It is mine! What is it?"

It was a mirror.

"Look! A shower-back!" they all shouted. "Merquzaq was at a trading-post and has brought strange things with him!"

They laughed, and kept saying that Neqe was now a place as rich in possessions as the white men's ships, and they all crowded around Ivalu to see their own faces. But, when they looked into the mirror, they saw the faces of those standing next to them, and they laughed even more.

Like a little queen Ivalu immediately stretched out her hand for her rare possession, and said it was a present for her and not for them. She wanted to have her envied treasure and wanted to go into the house and play with it alone.

So she went in and looked into the wonderful glass. It felt like ice but it didn't get wet when she put her hand on it. But suddenly she noticed that it *did* melt, and it looked different and didn't show her face any more. When she touched it with her fingers, it was damp. She got scared of the beautiful thing she had received and ran outside and called.

"Grandmother! Grandmother! Come to me! The mirror wants to melt! The ice wants to become water!"

They all called to her to bring it outside, that such things cannot stand going into warm houses. But Ivalu didn't want to bring it.

"It doesn't matter," she said. "My grandfather has brought me other things. He has many things in his sack!"

Ama was not certain whether the mirror should remain outside in the cold, but now she saw that it lay on the bed and was full of drops of water that could be wiped off. Now she understood. It only happened because it was cold. It was not ice, but something hard, of the nature of stone. Stones always did that. They covered themselves with frost and got wet when one took them into the house in the winter. She taught the little girl that heavy things did this out of anger, because they were removed. A stone wishes to lie still, and that was why, when he was taken into the house, he became different.

After Merquzaq had brought in all his things, he told his wife of the unusual houses which he had found up in the north. All sorts of possessions were crowded in the house. He had brought along a few jackets, and in the boxes he had tea and sugar. He also had brought a big kettle. This he had buried deep in the tea, so no one could see it. Now they brought it out and poured out the tea. Ama filled the kettle with ice and hung it over her lamp. As the water was boiling, Merquzaq stepped in front of his house and called to his friends to come in.

"One hasn't seen your faces for a long while," he said, "come in and visit! One longs to hear your sensible talk and to learn from your experiences!"

As they entered, they saw the big kettle hanging over the lamp and heard the boiling sound in it. He also had two cups, which he had never before had in the house. Now Ama poured hot tea from the nose of the kettle and she poured something from a box into it that looked like white sand and which sweetened the drink.

"Tea," she said. "Maybe you would like to drink some tea?"

Ama was like her husband. Now she talked as if tea was one of the things which was an everyday matter with people.

"Ak, yes, one has brought a little tea from his supply," said Merquzaq, and then he took the first cup and drank a swallow. Then he passed the cup to the next one, and he took his swallow. The tea was boiling hot and sweet and tasted as if one were on a ship and were given food by the cook, after one had traded and delivered many skins.

Merquzaq took the second cup, drank one swallow, and let it be passed around. This was really a house in which there were many possessions of the white men. Now and then Ama reached out, took the cups from the men and said. "Ak! I forgot to sweeten your drink!" And she put in more of the white stuff and stirred it for some time before she returned the cups.

After they had drunk for a while, Merquzaq refused to drink more. "One has become tired of always the same food," he said, and the others looked at him respectfully. They were very pleased at having been allowed to taste the unusual drink.

After nothing was left in the kettle, they wanted to talk and hear news, but Merquzaq lay down on his bed and began to sleep.

"Ak! a miserable man is without strength," he said. "Let us try to see if we can sleep."

Ama put fresh ice into her kettle and hung it over the lamp.

"It is possible," she said, "that the women might want tea, if they are not too full."

At this the men looked at each other. In this house no man could argue when the woman made them understand that further hospitality would be meant for others.

"Events have so shaped themselves that one must go," they said, one after another, and left.

"Ak! Are you going?" said Ama. Merquzaq
was asleep.

After the men had left, the grandmother took a
spoon and gave Ivalu one teaspoonful of sugar after
another. It tasted better than she believed anything
could taste. Ivalu put her fingers deep into the sugar
so that it reached high up over her arm. Then she
filled her hands with it, closed the mand let it run
through her fingers. She took some of it with the
spoon, poured it into the hollow of her hand, and let
it dribble down over the side. Then she ate again.
It was the most amusing game she had ever played.

"Ivalu! Ivalu! Come and play with us," the children called to her on the next day.

"I won't come out! I am playing in my house,"
she called back. Every time they came in for her she
sat near her box with the white wonder. When meat
was cooked, she did not want to eat.

"My mouth wishes the sweet," she said, and they
laughed and let her have her way. She did not eat
any meat in the evening either, although they told
her it was muskdeer, frozen muskdeer which her
grandfather had brought from across the sea. But she
got angry and said that what she ate was also brought
from across the sea, and that she did not want any
muskdeer meat.

But, as night came, she had a stomachache. She
called her grandmother and said she must go out,

but she became sick instead. At this the grandmother laughed very much and said Ivalu was like a newborn baby, and got sick if she had anything but milk. But Ivalu started to cry till they gave her the spoon and asked her if she wanted more sugar. She said yes, and ate again and again.

Her stomachache got worse and worse, and they understood that the white stuff in the box was avenging itself. Then they said she could eat bear meat, which gives people peace in their intestines. But Ivalu didn't care if she got stomachache, and, when the others wanted to drink tea, she even held the cover of the box tight and didn't want to allow them to take any of the white sand from it. At first they laughed, but Ivalu became angry and cried. So they all drank tea which was not sweetened, but the visitors wished that the little girl had much less to say.

Then came a day when there was almost nothing in the big box any more. Ivalu sat there with her spoon and complained.

"Ak! why did I have to be in such a hurry to eat it all! If I had eaten only a little every day, the box would never have become empty."

"If you got something again, would you then put it away and eat only a little at a time?" asked the grandmother.

"Yes," said Ivalu, "then I would see that something would always be left over."

The grandmother then brought out from under her skin covers a bag full of sugar which she had hidden. She laughed and said she had filled it while Ivalu was asleep, and that they would all divide this and only use it to sweeten the tea.

But Ivalu belonged to those who follow only their own wishes. When, one day, her grandmother had gone to the mountains to set snares for rabbits, the little girl again had the desire to eat sugar. She took the bag, and, when her grandmother returned, she found her little grandchild bathed in tears, for now there was nothing left any more. But Ama laughed and said she was glad only children had so little sense. Older people are wiser, and put things away, and therefore one must be pleased that the young ones, little by little, grow up.

For a long time Ivalu was troubled by the lack of sugar. The grown-ups, however, were more pleased over their good catches, for to them meat, and meat only, was the really tasty food. . . .

The spring wanted to push against the summer. The whole fjord was still covered with ice, but the water was cutting big rifts in it. In the places where the rivers streamed down from the mountains, shallows were created near the shore, so that it was difficult to get out to the ice. The men brought home much meat and Merquzaq caught many bearded seals and soon would be able to stretch large quantities of straps to dry.

He had no gun, but he was very capable when it came to harpooning the seals. He hid the harpoon between his knees so that the seals couldn't see it when he sneaked up on them. Whenever they lifted their heads to look around, he thrashed around with his knees so that the seals thought it was one of their number who was keeping watch, and they went back to sleep. But suddenly they felt a harpoon in the back, and even if they threw themselves into the breathing hole to flee, they were still held by a line and that terrible pain in the back. In the end, they had to come in the breathing hole to get air, and there Merquzaq stood waiting and killed them.

At times he didn't even use a harpoon, but crawled right up to the seals. Then, when they awoke, a man was lying over the breathing hole, and they got so frightened they forgot to fight and defend themselves.

Chapter Four

THE little auks began to arrive. They come only when the world is again light and the weather is mild. They will not live there otherwise. Mornings they swarm in from the sea with a rustling sound, like that of an iceberg overturning, and high above, like a cloud, one can see the hundreds upon hundreds which are on their way even further north. They scream down at the people, who stand and watch them as they pass over the settlement. At night, after the sun has crawled down behind the mountains, they fly back out to sea, and the mountains are still again.

Ivalu and her playmates sat on the rocks and watched everything around them come alive with the settling birds. Ama and some other women had built a hiding-place of stones on the side of a hill, and here they sat, waiting. They had nets tied to the ends of long poles, and these they swung through the air, catching the birds as they flew by in huge numbers. The children caught many of them, too, for many of the auks came to rest on the ground, and crawled under rocks to hide. When the children found them, they would reach in after them, and the little birds would peck at their fingers, thinking to defend themselves. But the youngsters managed to catch a great many, this way.

Evenings, when the older people cooked, the little ones came and put the birds which they had caught into the pots. The grown-ups told them that their catch tasted much better than those netted by the old women, and the children boasted that they, too, were big providers, and were now grown up and important.

Merquzaq brought in seals from the ice, and the children watched him skin the animals through their mouths. He pulled his sleeves up to his shoulders. Then, with a knife in his hand, he put his arm deep inside the seal, and by twisting the knife he cut the body free from the hide. This left only a thin sheet of blubber on the skin after he had pulled the seal through its own mouth. It was wonderful to see the seal "spit itself out", as Merquzaq called it.

Ama took all the auks she had caught and killed them quickly by pressing her finger against the chest bone and pushing the heart to one side. She folded their wings back and twisted them around one another. Then she stuffed them into the seal skin so they would lie in the blubber and grow tasty by winter.

Every once in a while Ivalu would run to her grandmother with a bird she had caught, but Ama said she should stay away or her running around would frighten the birds and they would not come close enough to be caught.

"Are they afraid of me, too, grandmother?" Ivalu asked. She felt very grown up and important because something living was afraid of her. "Look—I have caught two birds. Will you put them into the seal so I can eat them in the winter?"

Ama took the birds and bit off their feet, so that in the winter Ivalu would recognize them as the ones she had caught all by herself.

When the birds were numerous, Ama would sit with her net from early morning until late at night, and she was so clever that she could catch enough in two days to fill a seal skin. But on these days, when Ama was gone all day, Ivalu was lonesome for her grandmother, because when it was time to eat she had to eat out of the pots of others.

The people moved into huts and the houses were cleaned. The window skins and door flaps were taken down so that the dogs could run in and out and scratch off everything that had accumulated under the bed during the winter. This was fine for the bitches, and the young dogs which were not yet old enough to be broken to harness, as these were not kept tied, like the huskies.

On the walls of all the houses were bone hooks, which had been inserted between the stones when the houses were built. On these, in the winter, the people hung meat which was to be thawed out, but now the children used them to play their "hanging game". Orfik helped them, but he told them it was very dangerous.

"When one has hung somebody," he said, "Death will think the child has been hung up for him, and will quickly start to take hold of its legs. So one must take it down quickly, and then Death will be disappointed and will run away. He will learn that he has no power here."

They hung one another by their fur cowls, and they had to climb up on one another to reach the hook. When one had hung there for a moment, he forgot everything and it was just as though one were asleep. Then the others quickly took him down, and he could not stand on his feet, but fell down unconscious. After he had lain there a while, he would yawn, and when he began to blink his eyes, they all laughed at him. It was wonderful, for they always dreamed that they ate good things and smelled good smells, and their bodies felt good, just like when they had eaten a lot of delicious blubber.

But sometimes they made a mistake and let their playmate hang too long. Then he would get sick, but they all laughed just the same, and still everyone wanted to be the next to be hanged. They would scream with joy and shout, "Now it is my turn! Now hang me!"

When Ivalu was taken down and woke up, she said she dreamed she was grown up and had married a white man and possessed everything in the world, which one could wish for.

When she told this to the other children, they laughed at Ivalu and told her she would never marry a white man.

"When you are big," Orfik said, "then you shall be my wife. I shall take you on long catching trips, and I will give you many skins to scrape for me."

"I don't want to be big and I don't want to marry," Ivalu said. "That was only something my tongue said. I always want to stay with my grandmother."

But the others still laughed at her, so she ran away from them and hid by herself. She could hear them still at their game, shouting, "Now it is my turn! I want to be hanged now! It's my turn!"

Her grandfather was home and she ran to him for comfort. She told him she didn't want to play any more, because when she was hanged she dreamed that she was married to a white man, and then all the others laughed at her. Her grandfather stroked her head, and then he took a seal which he had just brought home, and pushed out its eye. He cut holes in it, and, holding it over Ivalu's mouth, he pressed out the sweet liquid. It tasted wonderful, and she immediately forgot all about the children's teasing.

A few days later the first summer storm came hissing down from the glacier. The women stayed in

their tents and were afraid, while the men ran back
and forth, lashing their catch straps around the tents
and weighting the ends with big rocks. After Ivalu
had listened to it for a while, she got sleepy. She
wasn't afraid of the storm, because she was with her
grandmother.

When she awoke, the sun was shining again. The
last of the ice was gone and the seals lay on the land
and everything was new and wonderful. The waves
were small and friendly as they were still young and
had not yet had time to grow into big ones. Orfik said
that last year he saw waves so big that they sent
white foam all the way to the cliffs and drove rocks
back and forth along the shore.

The children ran around on the rocks, spearing
for fish with little lox spears. The fish were very difficult to catch, as they were small and swam so fast.
Whenever they managed to catch some they ate
them alive, while they were still flopping. They had
a taste which was altogether new after their food of
the winter. At low tide the women and children
gathered mussels around the seaweed. They cooked
the mussels and made a soup which was quite sweet,
and reminded Ivalu of the sugar her grandfather had
brought home from his trip.

The *kayaks* were brought out and the men went
out hunting. Ivalu decided that she did not want to
be a woman any more, that she would rather be a

man and have a *kayak* to paddle and be able to stay away for a few days. Then, when she returned home, she could show off with a narwhal or a walrus, and all the people would come out and shout that there was catch again, and they would have a big feast. It must be very pleasant to be the one who says, "Here— please eat some of my meat. It is a pleasure to be able to please you"!

Little Ivalu was so silly. She always told everybody what she thought, and, when she told this to Orfik, he said that he was the one who would bring home meat, and she would just be his wife and would not have to worry about a *kayak*. He only said this because he himself could not go out with the others. He was a poor boy, who had to borrow a *kayak* from the other hunters when they wanted to sleep. Often they said "no", and then he had to stay home and just dream about going out.

And then, one day, the ship came! The great Peary could not stay away from the land of the people for any length of time. Whenever he left, he gave away a lot of presents, which made the people happy, but they were always afraid that they were farewell presents. When they asked him if he would return, he never said "yes" or "no", because Peary was a man who never made a promise which he could not be certain to keep.

It was Kullabak who first saw the ship from the hill, and she shouted so loud that her voice was heard even over the screaming of the auks. The people looked toward her and saw she was pointing out to sea. Then they, too, hurried up the hill, and from there they could see everything.

"Where is it going? If only it would come here!"

Ivalu was left behind. She could not run as fast as the grownups, and besides, she was wearing new boots which her grandmother had sewn out of beautiful white skins. They were so stiff that she couldn't bend her knees, and she began to cry. Then she saw that they had stopped and were looking out over the water, and, when she turned around, she saw the ship about which they were all making such a fuss.

Ak! it was only a tiny little one. She had thought it was going to be a big ship. Now she saw that it wasn't even as big as a little auk. She wanted to tell her grandfather to take his *kayak* and row out and bring it to her, so she could take it to bed with her and play with it on rainy days. Maybe there would be little white men on board, who could be her dolls.

The people noticed that the ship was trying to land at their settlement. At this they shouted even louder than they do when a hunter brings home the first narwhal of the year. The women laughed, joined hands, and danced around like children. They cried, "The white men will be welcome!" The men began to sing about how wonderful it would be to taste smoke again.

Merquzaq remained quiet. He felt that he was no longer the leaded of the people. For he used to travel with Peary, but now he was a little too old. And Peary was man who, from his first visit, picked out young men and brought them up and trained them. Now all those that he had chosen in the beginning were grown up, and he would have no need of any more older men.

As they approached the land, the white men stood high up on the ship. The anchor was slung to the ground and a heavy iron chain kept the ship from sailing away. Ivalu thought it must be wonderful to be a man who owned a *kayak*, and so could row over to the white man and shout to him that everybody was happy at the arrival of the ship.

The women stood in front of the tents and smiled. They told the children to be quiet, so they would not disturb the thoughts of the white men. The children jumped around their mothers and shouted, "Is the white man going to take more people along with him? Who is he going to take? Will he take me?"

Shortly after, the feared man landed. He had a black beard between his mouth and nose, but otherwise his face was smooth. His eyes always looked as if he was angry. His speech was peculiar; he spoke the language of the people as if he were a child. Without saying anything he pointed first at one, then at another. From this they knew they were being chosen to go with him, and then he told them that they were to come with him to the far north.

Ivalu had heard that he was a man who wanted to go to the place where the world had its belly-button. Maybe he wanted to look into it and find out strange things. They did not know what it was he wanted to do, but they knew he could take others along with him. Although it was a tiresome voyage, they wanted to go.

All the young men in the place were to go with Peary. As soon as they were chosen, their women began to shout with happiness and pack their things, for the white man had said he wanted to leave right away. The old people stood silent, and there was no joy on their faces because they could not go along. They said nothing, only stood there and hoped that their names would be called.

Suddenly Peary stepped over to Ivalu's grandfather and said, "Here I see the great Merquzaq."

"One is alive," Merquzaq said, "and one is well."

"You many seal straps?"

Merquzaq understood Peary's peculiar talk and said, "It happened accidentally that, in the spring, a miserable seal ran in my way."

"As usual," Peary said.

Merquzaq was silent, and he might well be, for

never before had he had as many straps as this year. His whole bed was made up of bundles of catch straps over which skins were spread. He had thought to present these to his fellow hunters, who had less luck with their seal catching than he. Whenever a man had no straps, he had to splice his catch line, and then it pleased Merquzaq to be able to give him a new one.

"Me no catch strap," Peary said.

"Come", Merquzaq said, and went into the tent. He, too, was a thinker and a leader, and here was even a white man following him into his tent to buy his possessions. Ivalu heard someone say that Merquzaq should have brought his straps outside, and not taken the white man into his tent.

"Admiration, as usual," said the white man, as Merquzaq pulled aside his bed skins and showed what he had.

"Here are your straps," he said, and looked pleased. "One would rather have grass as underskin for his bed. It is hard for an old man to sleep on skin straps."

The great man was one who thought of everything and he had decided to store meat some distance south of where he was going to spend the winter.

"Perhaps you come along and live at storing place?" he asked Merquzaq.

"Can a miserable man make decisions?" was the

answer. "Has my mouth the power of speech when you wish something?"

And so Merquzaq and all he possessed went along with the ship. It had been decided that he and four other families were to live in the place chosen by Peary for his caché camp. There they were to accumulate a great deal of meat, so that the sleds which would come down from the north the next spring could stop at their camp and be provided with dog food.

Meanwhile, the white men were walking among the tents, but they spoke a language which the people could not understand.

Ivalu was glad that she was still little and that nobody spoke to her, because she knew she would be speechless with fear and unable to answer, if they did. One tent after another was taken down, skins were put aboard, sleds, dogs, and all the possessions of the people. The ship was like a new land to which one moved. And as Ivalu saw old Ama packing her things, she got frightened, and told her grandfather she wanted her mirror and spoon. She thought that the white men would have respect for her if they saw she had possessions like theirs.

On board she saw peculiar things. The mast stood up to an immense height, and leading up to the point of the mast were straps so thick she could not close her fingers around them. A large number of white men were climbing up and down and were doing things, which must be very important. Before they did anything it was decided first, in that peculiar language, by one of them who was the master, and the others had to obey.

Soon the ship started. It felt as though it were trembling under the floor on which they were standing, and it sounded as though a lot of bears were hidden underneath and murmuring. But she noticed that nobody on board was worried, and over the high rail of the ship she could see the shore disappear. One was moving forward, but it did not tire one, and her grandfather told her that the ship had a tail like a whale and that was what made it go through the water.

After a while there was a call and she knew something was going to happen. It turned out that the cook had decided it was time for them to eat. It was all very strange. One sat up high near a raised thing, which was covered with heavy material, and there one ate things that were full of good taste but also others which made one sick. The great cook stood there with his assistants and watched their feasting. Men, women and children were served at the same time. Everyone had a cup, and a spoon which one used for those things which one could not hold in one's fingers.

Suddenly Ivalu got a pain in the mouth, but she did not dare to say so for fear of hurting the great cook's pride. So she went to the rail of the ship and spit everything into the water. The big cook saw it and said something but luckily he laughed and was not insulted. Shortly after that Ivalu got tea with sugar, and she thought of the days in the settlement when her mouth had always been sweet.

After they had been sailing a long time and the sun was in front of the ship, it was decided that they should sleep. All the people were put in a large bed where they lay in long rows. Soon they were all asleep, because all the things which they had seen had made their eyes tired. Perhaps Ivalu was the only one whose interest in the things around her would not cease. She lay between her grandparents, so she was not afraid. After she had lain there a long time she had to go out. She didn't dare call her grandmother, for her speech would insult those on the ship. It was best that only people who could speak the white man's language should talk. Finally, she slipped out of her grandmother's arms and got up.

There was only one small window, and toward this she started, but she did not know that it was dangerous to walk around in the dark. Suddenly she felt as though she had stepped into emptiness, and fell to the bottom of the ship. She had hurt herself, and she was frightened, but she lay quiet and did not cry. There were no people there, and from this she knew she was in a part of the ship where no one was supposed to be. She looked for a way out. She had fallen into a space with piles of coal on all sides, and, when she tried to move, coal rolled down from every direction. There was no door.

She looked all around, but the walls were made of wood and there were no holes through which one could look out. It was so dark, and now she cried hard, but she tried to hold back her sobs so nobody would hear her. The silent tears ran down her cheeks. She wiped them off and her hands got wet, and in the little light she could see she had gotten all black and dirty from the coal. She began to shiver from the cold, and thought that maybe she had fallen through a crevasse in the ship, like the ones in the glaciers, and that this one had dropped her into the underworld, where she now lay. She began to be afraid she would never see her grandmother again, and she cried harder. But, after a while, she thought it might be better to wait and see what would happen, and she sat there very quietly until she heard one of the people upstairs calling, "Ivalu! Where is little Ivalu?"

It was the voice of her grandmother. Then someone else spoke, and she could hear them all talking about her disappearance, and she heard them tell the white men that she was missing. She was terribly afraid, because now she felt even more that nobody was allowed to be down there where she was.

Suddenly she saw that a cover over her head was being pulled back. That was where she had stepped, thinking it was part of the floor, and where she had slid down. Two white men pulled it aside, and then she could hear her grandmother crying that her little grandchild must have fallen overboard and been drowned. The two men bent over the edge and peered down. Ivalu looked up and was afraid of their anger, so she kept very quiet. But one of the men saw her eyes gleaming, like stones in the sand. He shouted a few words and they all crowded around and looked down at her.

Ak! how frightened she was, and how ashamed of her behavior! She grew even more terrified when one of the men came down in the hole to get her. He would kill her for what she had done—and she was so scared she didn't dare to cry! The man took her under his arm and carried her up. He climbed to the deck, holding her tight, and Ama came running and crying happily that her little grandchild wasn't dead. Several white men came up and she was sure she was going to be killed, for they talked a lot and pointed at her. She decided to cry, so that they would have mercy on her, but at that moment a door in the wall opened and the great man stepped out—Peary himself was walking toward her.

Peary and the man who had rescued her talked a great deal in the language which she could not understand. Again she became silent with fear, for she thought that if he bothered with people at all, it was only to decide whether they should live or die. He took her in his arms and carried her from one of the little houses into another. He carried her through a narrow passage and into a little house that had a big pot in it, and in which he made water run from the wall!

"He wants to boil me," Ivalu thought. But she saw no fire and then she knew that she was to be drowned.

"I must have come to the end of my life," she thought as she was placed in the water. But dying was different from what she had thought, because the water was quite warm and seemed as soft as down. Then the big man took something which was smooth and pink-colored, ·which the white men use to rub down their skin. It foamed all over her body as though the sun were shining on her belly and warm winds were blowing on it. Then she was put back into the water, and she understood that Peary was asking for something which was not there.

Ama came in with another old woman and they chattered and laughed and said that Ivalu should be grateful to the big white man for paying any attention to her. But Ivalu only thought that he wanted to have her body white and nice tasting before he began to eat her. Then he took her out of the water and rubbed her with a piece of white material. She saw that her skin had become white. Was he trying to make her over into a little white girl? She was put down on Peary's own narrow bed, where there was room for only one person, and then she was covered with a sack full of feathers. Ivalu was happy. Her eyes closed, and she felt she was going to sleep in a place which was meant for a white man only—a white man, who was master over a whole ship.

Chapter Five

AK! these great white men on the ship! Now one could learn what they were like, and one had much to learn, for they had, indeed, strange customs and ideas.

One found out, too, that in the land of white men Peary had to serve an even greater man than himself, a leader to whom the white men brought all their catch. Ak! one's head might split from trying to think of a man so great that he could think even for Peary, and who spoke words which Peary must obey!

Merquzaq, who was one of the wisest men in the world, reported that this great leader of the white men wanted to eat animals which were caught away up on the navel of the world, and that was why white men were sent there, and used the people as guides. Peary was this greatest master's assistant, and that was why he was the leader on this boat which had been sent to the north. Also, the great white master wanted to see all the lands there were, but his own important hunting made it impossible for him to go and visit them himself. So he sent out wise white men to make drawings of the land for him to look at. One could see, from the fact that they used certain instruments, that they also wanted to find out the relation of the sun to the different lands.

Sometimes they would go on long sled journeys on which they would not even take time to determine either the hunting conditions or the kind of game along the way. They only travelled, and ate pemmican, and were always hungry and tired and sleepy.

Peary, or the man to whom he had given the leadership of that group, was always in the lead. As soon as it was barely dawn, he would get up and wake all the others with the shout: "Adolo! Adolo!" Then they all had to get up and the ride began.

The energy of the white men was like a sickness which finally infected the whole party. Often the dogs and men were driving themselves beyond the limits of strength. But sometimes, after one of these terrific efforts, they would find that all they had done was to get over a pack-ice mound, and were standing facing another!

Peary was a forceful man and his will was so strong that he accomplished things which seemed impossible. Only on one occasion had Death, whom he so often provoked, almost caught up with him. A bear who hated the people turned from his seal-hunting and dug up the supplies which Peary had stored for the return trip. The animal ate all the food, and, as they had run into a snowstorm and were forced to make camp there, starvation nearly took their lives.

And then there was the time when Manizok reached the end of his strength and it was impossible for him to go further. They could spare him only one dog leg for food, so they left him with it in a snow hut, and beat their way through to the ship. They arrived nearly exhausted, and none of them was capable of making the return trip to rescue Manizok. But Peary stayed for only one meal on the ship, and then, alone, forced his way back and found Manizok. He had eaten the dog leg, and was alive, but his eyes had frozen and, when they brought him back on the sled, his eyes were all grey and life did not wish to come back into them. The people pitied him in his blindness, and Merquzaq went to comfort him in his misery.

"Life is big and eyes are only very little," the old man said. "They are the price you had to pay for your life, this time. Do not worry. There are many people who will take care of you and see that you always have enough meat."

The people all told Manizok that these were wise words, and finally Manizok did not regret the loss of his eyes any more. When they saw that he was not going to worry and complain and be a burden, Merquzaq said they should pick a woman for him upon whom he could lean in his helplessness, and that he should be married soon. "One must find a clever woman to look after his house," Merquzaq told them.

At this Manizok smiled, and Ivalu realized that

life is not without happiness for those who cannot see. She had never before thought of this, but gradually she became wiser and every day she was experiencing things which taught her more and more about the world.

The white men did not know everything. Often the people laughed at their ignorance, and particularly when they tried to ride over the trackless snow with their dogs, in places where the dogs did not want to go.

One day Ivalu and another little girl went over the ice to play. They heard a lot of shouting near by, and saw a sled rushing toward them, pulled by galloping dogs. A man sat on the sled and swung a whip in a strange manner. The dogs howled whenever he managed to hit them, but that happened seldom. The next moment the sled was right in front of them. Here the dogs stopped and would go no farther.

The children saw that the dogs had been pulling the sled in a direction contrary to the will of the driver. They saw that he was one of the big white men, the one who always stayed on the ship and was ready in case someone should get ill. He was a dispeller of pains, and did not go on the long trips or hunt. One saw him live on things placed in front of him at the table, but he never brought anything home himself.

Ak! how angry he was. He evidently forgot that his own ignorance was the cause of the dogs' behavior. They only felt good, and were testing their strength against that of the man who was supposed to guide them. Now he took his whip, jumped forward between the animals, and with the handle beat their heads and necks. But he hit only two of the howling animals before the handle broke, and then he had no whip any more.

Again he shouted strange words, and jumping back to the sled he pulled out the harpoon from under the lacing and began a merciless beating of the dogs. The children were terrified that in his anger he might kill some of the dogs and then it would be their turn. But the dogs became panicky under the beating and jumped around so that the harness became twisted in his legs and he fell full length on the ice. The little girls did not laugh as they would have if the dogs had run away from one of their own people. The white man's mouth was a waterfall down which poured terrible anger. He completely forgot that the little girls were watching him as he lay on the ice and howled in fury at the dogs. Then he freed himself from the tangle of harness and ran to the ship, with the children right behind him. They were just in time to see how he was received by his companions, and none of them were laughing. They all talked at once, and very loudly—that was all.

That evening, when Ivalu told her grandmother about the funny thing she had seen, old Ama explained to her that in the land of the white men one could be a great master without knowing how to harness a dog. Their wisdom was so great that they could make food come up out of the earth—food which did not have to be killed. They made little holes in the ground, and out of these holes the power of the white man made food come right up into the air. So one must never laugh at a white man, because he was master over many things about which the people understood nothing.

One day Peary called several of the people to him and told them that he was bound to reach the navel of the world and that nothing must stop him. The weather, during the past year, had been bad, so he had been unable to reach his goal. Merquzaq, in his own mind, knew that the world was ashamed and didn't want to show herself as she really was. That was why she sent storms and bad sled roads. It was only to keep the white man from the place which nature had decided they must not reach.

"One more year I have," Peary said. "Not much food to eat. Many people, little time; few people, long enough."

It was clear to them that Peary was behind in his plans, and had to make a decision: either he had to return home quickly or feed fewer people. So it was decided that Merquzaq, Manizok, and a party large enough to fill eight sleds with women and children, should return home. That way their mouths would not eat the food needed by those really necessary to the undertaking.

They were happy over the prospect of the journey. Here, where the white men's ship was, there was no bird-hill, and many of the women were longing for little auks so that they could chew the skins for shirts for the children. This was pleasant work for old women whose teeth had become flat and short. Then, too, there was too much talk which the men had to obey. And they said that although they were glad to be with Peary, this long period of happiness was tiring. It would be nice to be doing something useful again, and not just be satisfied with making difficult trips at the end of which there was not even the pleasure of a big catch.

When they were all ready to go except for waiting while the women assembled all the things which they had forgotten, Peary came out, took Ivalu by the hand, and led her into his own little house on the ship.

"Ak! if he will only decide to let me stay with him for always," Ivalu thought. "Maybe he will let the others leave, and keep me here and then take me back with him to his great lands. Maybe I am a daughter whom he left here to grow up, and be a

surprise to his countrymen when he takes me back
home!"

Peary put a wonderful closed box in front of her,
brought biscuits, and gave her a lot of the sweet
food which she liked so well. It was evidently his intention that she alone should remain on the ship with
him and be his daughter. She seemed to belong there,
anyway, for whenever she played she thought only
of white men and always wanted to be the wife of a
white man. Now she had become one—!

She forgot to eat, but the great man broke the biscuits and put them into her mouth. When he did
this, her lips touched his fingers and she thought this
was wonderful. It was as though one were tasting
with *his* mouth instead of one's own, and now she
was sure he must be her father.

"You eat," Peary smiled at her.

She began to stuff the food into her mouth, but
it still seemed too slow for him. "Do quick," he said,
and then he took her hand, put the box under her
arm, and led her out.

Ak! it was clear now that he did not intend to
keep her there at all, or hide her from the others.
He led her to Merquzaq's sled, lifted her up, and
stroked her cheeks. She could say nothing, for inside her she wanted to cry. Ak! she was really to
leave. Slowly she thought with anger of a snow hut,

and she decided that what she wanted was to live on a ship forever.

How stupid it sounded when grandfather cracked his whip and shouted "Hock! Hock!" to the dogs! The animals howled and the sleds began to move. Away over the land they went, across a mighty sea to the other shore where it looked as though the earth had fleas, so many rabbits were swarming over the bare patches of ground. They shot great numbers of them, but Ivalu would not eat any.

One day she realized that she hated her grandfather as he sat on the front of the sled, cracking his whip and forcing her to go further and further away from the ship. She sat between her grandparents, and every minute Ama put a skin over her to protect her from the wind. But Ivalu sulked and kicked the skins aside, and finally did not even answer them when they spoke to her. But, in the evening, a snowstorm started, and it was hard to throw off the skins with which her grandmother had covered her.

"Ak! the poor child," Ama said. "She has to go forward on a long sled journey while her thoughts are always going further backward. One feels sorry for the person one would help most."

Ivalu still would say nothing but she understood that her grandmother meant well by her. It was comforting to be the object of so much attention, even if one couldn't have exactly what one wanted most. No one could be as good as her grandmother.

And so they travelled until summer came and the ice broke up. They had reached a place where the catching was good and here they put up their tents. They stayed throughout the summer, and in the fall they continued their journey. At last they reached a place where, Merquzeq said, they were to cross the sea into their own and. It was stagnant ice, difficult to cross, so the women took the children's hands and helped them over. Often, on this long journey, they were without food and the children had nothing to eat. The men were more concerned about moving forward than living in comfort on the way.

Once, when they came to a halt, one of the women looked down at the many little footprints which marked the trail of the children in the snow.

"Ak! when I look at the little feet which made those prints, then the tears want to come in my throat," she said. "We who live here in the north have been born in a land full of hardships. Think of these little children who have to go through the whole darkness before light comes again!"

"Yes," said another woman, "it is very strange that of all the peoples in the world, we live in the farthest north, where there is nothing but darkness and cold."

But at this Merquzaq stepped up to them and said:

"It is a wonder to me that I listen to women's talk, but still I want to say this: you must not feel sorry for these children because they have to walk so far. Through this they become accustomed to hardships from childhood, and so are made capable of living the life which people who live in these parts must endure. I want to ask you all—is there any place you would want to change for this, or where you would rather live?"

At this all the women said "no", they lived in the best place in the world. The men laughed a little, quietly, because they felt that what the women said was true.

Chapter Six

YEARS pass, and children grow up. Ivalu now played older games, some of which took her far out on the fjord ice or over the land. She helped Ama in many things. Sometimes she scraped the blubber off the sealskins, and at others she sat on the hill and caught little auks. But, if she got tired of work, she would simply drop it and run with the others, for she never got tired of playing.

Ivalu had grown up and the young men were beginning to notice that her body was becoming desirable and her smile inviting. Her breasts were beginning to rise under the tight fitting shirt of birdskin. Many young men came to her settlement to see her, but they always pretended that they were only passing on their way North or South, or were just anxious to see new faces. Ivalu's life was a continuous game. It was a game to sit on the hill and watch over the narwhal meat which had been put out to dry, because then the boys would come up and tell her all about their great experiences while hunting. Her girl friends, too, were very respectful, even though their fathers had more meat for drying.

She would cut the meat into thin slices and lay them in the sun so they would dry on both sides. Now and then she would cut off a piece of blubber and contemptuously throw it away. The boys would shout that they were her dogs, who were fighting for a bite, and then they would fight to see who would receive the piece of blubber. The lucky victor would look at Ivalu to see if she had noticed he had got it. And Ivalu found that she could even make them eat rancid blubber, and all sorts of foolish things. If it just came from her hand they seemed to value it.

That winter Ivalu frequently slept in the house of the boys. They were full of the strength and vigor of life. Then, too, the older people talked only of ordinary, everyday things which the youngsters (in their own opinion) understood much better than their parents. Ama told Ivalu that in her young days it had been exactly the same. Then she, too, thought it was ridiculous to sit around and talk over the soling of boots. But now she was old, and the many boots which she had sewn had trodden ground in many lands, but still she wanted every new little wisdom which she could get from others.

"Ak!" Ivalu said, "sewing tires me. I don't want to watch the lamps for any man."

She ran out and told her playmates that her grand-father had some wonderful rotted walrus skin, and she was going to take a piece of it. So they all ran into the house of which they had taken possession.

"Ak!" the older people said, "they are little men and women, who are practicing married life."

They laughed and said that their old age would

be taken care of as long as they had healthy children to continue the family and bring catch into the house.

One day it happened. It was the usual thing in the life of a woman, but something of which Ivalu had never thought. Mitzerk came to the settlement —the capable, gay Mitzerk, who always was lively and talkative and had quick, unexpected answers for all questions.

He arrived by sled. Most of his dogs were black, and even though there were not many of them they were well trained and fast. He came from the North, and his fame had preceded him. He had killed a huge bear, the first one he had ever faced, single-handed. The skin lay rolled up on the sled and pieces of meat stuck out on all sides. The tremendous shanks of the animal were longer than the crosspieces of his sled. He whirled up to the settlement and, as Ivalu looked at him standing there, his long hair all around his head and hanging into his eyes, she began to think. His hairband was a sealskin belt, and his clothes were worn. He was a man without a woman, a man who went on dangerous trapping trips. He was a man whose clothes were carelessly patched, and always by other men's wives.

She passed by his dogs, walking a little stiffly and slowly, pretending she had something important to do on the hill. After she had walked out of his sight

she stopped for a minute to set her fur cowl right.
Ak! now she was sorry she had not sewn the tear
in her seal jacket about which her grandmother had
spoken to her a long time ago. She was a little
ashamed that she had nothing to do at the hill, and
went back to the house.

Mitzerk had unharnessed his dogs and began to
build himself a tent. So—he wanted to remain here
a few days and sleep in his own house? She stopped,
but only for a moment, and looked at the load on his
sled. When she noticed that he stopped his work in
order to look at her, she threw her head back, turned
around, and went home. Her grandmother was at-
tending to the lamps.

"One remembered something one had forgotten,"
Ivalu said. "Is there any thread in the little box?"

"Do you want to sew?" Ama asked. "Here, let
me fix your coat."

Ivalu took off her jacket and her grandmother
sewed it so that it was once more whole and neat.
Ivalu always took care to be well dressed, even though
the other women looked sloppy. Big girls are a drain
on their father's catches if they always want fine
skins to dress in. Let them wait until they are married, their fathers would tell them, and then their
husbands can show off their prowess as trappers
through their well dressed women.

A little while before, a white whale had been caught in the ice, and Merquzaq had brought home the back tendons. They were to be split and dried, and Ivalu took the thread box and sat out in the open. In many places the greed of the sun had eaten the snow away, and she sat on the cliff with the box in her lap. She split the sinews into fine threads which were to be used to fasten boot soles and to sew mittens for the hunters.

The children ran playing around Mitzerk's sled. The larger boys took their knives and cut slices off the tempting frozen bear meat and ate them. There were also a few young girls gathered around him, but Ivalu had no desire to join them. She sat there, a busy woman splitting the sinews and rolling the thread against her wide cheeks with the flat of her hand. Then she stretched the sinews tight and set them in the sun, and soon they were dry and stiff and something for a woman who takes pride in her sewing to look at.

Heia—ja—ja! Suddenly she saw Mitzerk come toward her tent! One could see he had a little bundle in his hand, but Ivalu got up and went in to her grandmother. Strange, she had been thinking of him and now he came. When he came into the tent she did not even look up, she was very busy picking needles from her sewing box on the bed.

"Ak! one thought there were people here," Mitzerk said. "Now one sees that he was mistaken, and there are only women."

Ama said nothing, and as Ivalu was young she kept quiet. Mitzerk remained standing for a while. He moved his hand with the bundle and they could see it was strips of bear skin.

"One has accidentally come to the settlement," he said.

"Ak! has someone really arrived? Joy for us who live here!" Ama said.

"Where is Merquzaq?" the young trapper asked, to justify his being there. "I see his dogs are tied outside."

"He is digging meat holes on the hill of many stones," Ama said.

At this he left. Ivalu could tell from his face that he had wanted to deliver his package, and she was pleased that his embarrassment had made him shy and humble. That night her sleep was troubled, and the next day she did not go out to play with the others. Instead, she lay on the bed and thought about Mitzerk, and the fact that when he saw them he had so little to say. Then she thought of his dogs, and remembered everything about his sled, and she thought it strange that suddenly she should be so interested in the property of somebody else.

Mitzerk had let it be known that that night he wanted everyone to come and eat his bear meat. But although the others went, Ivalu undressed and lay on the bed, and did not go out to Mitzerk's feast.

The following day he again came to the house. His tent was up now, so he was settled there and a neighbor. He came in humbly, like a trapper who is seldom fortunate enough to bring home meat.

"It happened that one encountered a little meat," he said, and laid it on the side plank.

"Aye," Merquzaq said. "Did you shoot the bear —as usual?"

"Ak! no," Mitzerk said. "Not as usual, but at last."

The others looked at each other and smiled, shaking their heads over his fine modesty.

"One would wish that these miserable stocking edgings be scraped and dried," Mitzerk said, and laid down a few skin strips on which there was long bear hair. It was the mane of the big male bear he had killed—the coveted long, mane hairs, which all women want for stocking edgings.

"One has cut them by accident," he said. He did not want to admit that he had intentionally lowered the value of the skin. "Perhaps they will be scraped and dried in this tent."

Ama looked at her grandchild questioningly.

"Pah!" Ivalu said. "As if one wished to scrape skins for a traveller! Let those prepare his catch who need to do it!"

Without looking at any one, she ran out of the tent. She saw one of her playmates and began talking about the snow sparrows, saying that there seemed to be a great many of them and soon, probably, all sorts of birds would come. She left her friend, after a little while, and walked far up the valley. She saw that the little saxifrage was beginning to break through the bare patches of ground, and would soon be up. Then she sat on a ledge and looked at the stream trickling down from the rocks above her. Soon she did not see these any more, and only sat there with her eyes wide open, staring into space. Here she sat for a long time until she was suddenly aware of what she was thinking. Nobody should ever say that Ivalu was thinking. She was only Ivalu, who sat waiting for someone to come again. Perhaps the great Peary would come and take her on another trip to the North. She would know much more than she had known the last time, when she was small and only wanted the white man to give her sweet things to put into her mouth.

The usual thing happened. Ivalu was a woman, and, when evening came and Mitzerk came to get her, she scratched him with her nails, bit his fingers, and cried and screamed so that the whole settlement could hear what was happening. While he was carrying her across the settlement, she noticed that nobody was openly looking, but heads were peeking out from behind tent flaps and meat piles. She saw the faces grinning while she was fighting her suitor, and even after the little tent flap had fallen behind them she could imagine the children standing in a group and pointing at Mitzerk's tent. Inside, her resistance lessened. Her strength was broken and he threw her so hard on the little bed that she fell. She remained lying with her knees bent and her face hidden in her arms, her body trembling lightly from her crying. Mitzerk sat there quietly and waited for words to come. But no words came.

After he had sat there for a while, he threw back the flap, went out, and sat on his sled with a file and a knife, fixing the point of his harpoon. He was filing, scraping and examining the point for all the world like a man fixing his weapons while his wife was busy inside. Pretty soon a man came along and stood beside him. Mitzerk paid no attention. The point of his harpoon was the only thing in the world that existed for him.

"Are you sharpening your harpoon?" the man asked. He, too, of course, had no idea that anything was going on.

"It is not impossible that one would like to have it a little different," Mitzerk said, and went right on filing.

He remembered that he had another file in the tent, which he could well use at the moment. If he only dared to call to Ivalu: "Listen, you in there—bring me my file—", then he would have shown the settlement that he was a man who could give orders. But he was too wise. He did not want anyone to be able to laugh at him, so he kept quiet and went on whittling the hard walrus tusk.

After the man had gone, three women came along. They, too, stopped and spoke a few words. But Mitzerk was a man who attended to his work and had no talk for women. They asked about something unimportant.

"One does not know. I do not know very much," he said, and did not even look up at them.

Shortly thereafter he went into the tent. Ivalu was sitting up, but bent over and pouting. He decided to test things and asked her to hand him his knife. She did not answer and remained motionless.

"One supposes that cooking should be done," Mitzerk said. But he was all alone in the tent. The young woman was deaf and dumb, and a little while passed in silence.

"Let us try to think," he said, finally, and bent over her to the lamp.

Ak! this lamp was just a miserable thing. Mitzerk was a young man who placed no value on household utensils, and it looked ridiculous as it stood there on three legs. It was the only preparation he had made for his marriage. Now he lighted some moss and poured a little something out of a tin can into the lamp; but, as he tried to bend over her knees, he stumbled involuntarily and it all fell over. He, himself, fell right into her lap.

"Ak! what a stupid!" she said, and gave him a push. And that was how their first contact was made. It started an argument between them, so that they fought back and forth, like all married people. In the beginning the quarrel was so loud that all their neighbors could hear it, but soon it died out. The night was long and both of them were young, and when they came out of their tent the next morning, Ivalu had been properly married.

She went down to the rocks and joined the children at their play, trying to act as though, after all, she was still one of them, and as though nothing had happened to make her any different from what she had been yesterday. When she got tired of running around, she went into her grandmother's house.

"One has gotten a desire to eat," she said, and taking some meat she chewed it with great appetite.

Ama scraped seal skins and talked with another woman, who had come visiting. No one mentioned that Ivalu was married—since two people's living together happens only to them, it is unnecessary to talk about it in front of many. In the corner lay the bearskin strips with the long hairs. They tempted Ivalu but she did not touch them. She was showing that no man had any influence on her, and nobody saw her go into Mitzerk's tent all that day.

In the middle of the day Mitzerk visited Merquzaq.

"One would wish to use your saw," he said. Merquzaq's tools were famous and always in order.

They were eating in the tent when he entered, and a piece of meat was handed to him.

"Are you going to catch?" Merquzaq asked.

"It is not impossible that one should try to make a little trip," he said, and no more was spoken. Merquzaq was eating, and a mouth only has one opening. Eating and talking each has its own time.

The weather was good and the sun lured seals out on the ice. But one waited until the sun was lower and then crawled out to the animals: so in the early evening Mitzerk took his sled and drove out. He did not say anything, and Ivalu wondered whether she was going to sleep in his tent or stay with Ama. Shortly afterwards Merquzaq and the other trappers started to go. Often, at this time, the women gather to talk about things which are not mentioned in the presence of men, then they sleep wherever they get sleepy. A woman without children is tied to no place.

From breathing hole to breathing hole Mitzerk drove, and as morning came and the sun stood high in the sky, his sled was so heavily laden that it was impossible to lash any more seals to the crossbars.

But there was one more seal to kill. He fastened it to the end piece of the sled and dragged it home behind his load.

The people gathered in a crowd as Mitzerk arrived.

"Ak! a mighty hand has been hunting," the boys shouted.

Mitzerk was glad that his dogs could not pull the seals across the melting ice wall to the beach. His whip cracked and his shouts were loud. The dogs howled and strained the harness taut, but the sled would not move. Finally he had to unload five seals.

Ivalu was in the crowd who stood near his sled. They were all shouting to him that seals would become scarce as a result of his tremendous catch.

"Ak! no, I am a miserable catcher with no knowledge of how to kill animals," he said. It was a triumph for him and a triumph for his young wife. Now, however, he was overdoing it, and he began to call to Ivalu. He even spoke her name and gave orders.

"Ivalu!" he shouted. "Bring my tarpaulin skins so I can spread them over these miserable seals!" He wanted to protect them from the sun so that the hairs would not loosen.

But this was too much.

"You stupid!" Ivalu said, and was embarrassed. "Ak! listen! Here, no doubt, is somebody talking!"

She was mocking him, and stood without moving behind the women, her hands in her boots.

"She is not bringing the sled cover," he said, and the others felt a quarrel, a test of strength. They watched and were pleased. Only Ivalu spoke a few words. They did not understand why, but she was embarrassed and had to tease him. Yet nothing happened. Mitzerk brought the sled cover himself, and then tied his dogs.

"Is meat cooked?" he asked, turning to the women. It was aimed at Ivalu.

Nobody answered, and Ivalu crossed the settlement with the children. She was not married, not she! She was taking care of no man!

"Meat was cooked in our tent," Ama said, trying to help her granddaughter. Mitzerk went to their tent and ate big pieces of meat and drank soup with them.

"It happens that one goes home," he said, and went out without looking about him.

For a few hours he sat there alone. Ak! how gladly would he have called his wife, but she had forgotten all about him and so he slept alone. When he awoke, he harnessed his dogs, swung his whip over the team and drove out on the ice. He noticed, however, that Ivalu stood there and looked after him.

Again he had a mass of seals on his sled, but this time he came home last. He had gone far out, and turned back only when it began to blow and all the seals slipped back into the water. He drove by the tents, to the hill, and, rolling huge rocks away, he built meat pits which he filled. Seal after seal he laid in unskinned, so that they would decompose deliciously. He thought of how, in the winter, his wife would sit on the bench and say, "Come on and eat! Eat our meat!" At the thought, he lifted even bigger rocks and soon he had many meat pits filled—dog fodder, and food for guests in the dark winter.

When he returned home, he was very tired. All the people were in their tents. His own tent was empty, so he went to Merquzaq's and there sat Ivalu and the others.

"It happens that one has returned," he said.

"Ai," Merquzaq said. "Have you returned? And have you caught?"

"I have no catch worth mentioning," Mitzerk said." I don't know how to catch. I am unsuccessful at my task."

"Ak, you poor man!" Merquzaq said, and laughed lightly.

Mitzerk felt he was a man. Ak, it was wonderful to be married. Now he could join in the general discussions, and could dominate the conversation. He drew himself up a little. His trousers were smeared with blood and his hands were red from the large numbers of seals he had killed. One could see from his clothes that he had crawled over the snow, and they were wet and torn. His hair was wild under his headband. Yes, here surely was a grown man and a trapper.

Ivalu looked at him and thought with pride that he belonged to her. And Mitzerk, after they had been eating for a while, decided the time had come.

"It happens that one goes," he said. "Come to the tent."

"Ak, listen to his talk!" Ivalu said. "Keep quiet, you, or speak to someone else."

Mitzerk turned and looked straight at her.

"Come now. One must go!"

He was talking directly at Ivalu and she had to obey.

"You are unpleasant to listen to," she said. "Wait a little. I am hungry and must eat."

Mitzerk sat down, scowling slightly. After Ivalu had eaten her piece of meat, she reached out for another. Mitzerk got up and spoke sharply.

"Come now. One goes immediately!"

Ivalu's grandparents were silent, and the visitors looked at the wall. Ivalu got up and went with him. Mitzerk was proud. A man was going home accompanied by his wife. They had been out visiting and now were going back to their own tent. Yes, a real married couple was walking through the settlement for everybody to see.

It was very windy the next day and nobody went out hunting. Ama came to visit them and brought a lamp, of which she had too many.

"One brings a bad thing," she said, and set it down. Ivalu wanted to thank her but it would have sounded too intimate, and as though she considered herself a part of Mitzerk's household. So she said nothing. When Ama left she knew she was a grandmother whose granddaughter had finally accepted marriage.

Ivalu quickly became a real wife. She gave up her playing and went home early to light her cooking lamp. Evidently, her abilities had only been concealed and unused. Now they were brought out, to her husband's advantage, and soon people saw that Mitzerk's wife was one of those who forgot to sleep when there was something to do. They were a fine couple— two young people with fast dogs, a lot of meat put by, even this early in the summer, and Ivalu had dried many skins to be used as boots for both of them.

One day visitors arrived, a group of young men from the Windside, who were driving from settlement to settlement merely for the fun of it. One of them was Orfik, and, when the other young men drove on to another settlement, he remained there. He was very capable, and often he brought home more seals than even Mitzerk. The people at whose tents he slept were happy about his catch. A young man who brings meat into the house is a welcome guest.

When it became late spring and the ice started to melt, the settlers distributed themselves, as usual, among the different places where they wanted to spend the summer. Mitzerk's two brothers joined the settlement, and also Manizok, who had gone blind. It was necessary to help him in many ways, but he was so goodnatured and patient that everyone liked having him as a neighbor. And he was capable. He let the dogs find a breathing hole, and stood with his harpoon, waiting. When the seals came up to breath, he could hear them, and he hunted that way. Orfik and he lived together.

Slowly the ice broke up. White whales came into the stretches of open water, and whaleskin became the food of the settlement. The women dried meat. One ate in the sun and slept in the sun, and the light was so bright it hurt one's eyes.

One morning, when Mitzerk got up, he found he was snowblind. He had been out longer than the others on the previous day, and he had slept only a short time in order to go right out again.

"When it is winter, darkness comes and then one can sleep," he had said, "and when I was a little boy I slept all the time. Now I can balance my life by hunting more and sleeping less."

But now his eyes ached. They felt as though they

were filled with sand which was burning into his head. He kept his face under the bed skins to avoid the rays of light that felt like knives being stuck into his brain. Ivalu sat by him and gave him meat, which he ate under the covers in the dark. Ama came to visit and sang a little song to cure his eyes, but her song was without power. The sun beat down on the tent wall and heated their little home. Mitzerk perspired under his many furs, panting and groaning.

Orfik came in and sat for a long time, and then Mitzerk heard a slight scuffling. He heard Ivalu say, "What is this? Let me go!" and he listened closely.

"Don't you hear me? Leave me alone!" Her voice was sharp but Orfik did not go. Mitzerk heard his young wife cry out again, and he understood Orfik desired her. He did not want to show himself stingy with his wife, for the others would say, "It is terrible how closely he figures with a woman!", but he forgot the pain in his eyes and started to uncover his head. At the first ray of light the knives again drove into his brain and he got back under the covers. Shortly after, Orfik and Ivalu went out, and the sick man was left alone.

The next day Orfik came again, and when he left Ivalu went with him. Mitzerk lay there for a long time, thinking that when a man is sick he should have attention from his wife without asking for it.

She was gone a long time, but he was a man who did not complain.

"One brings meat," Ivalu said. It was cooked meat which she had brought from Ama.

When he felt a little better and the sun was lower, he kept his head out of the covers and his eyes open. After a few days his eyes were all right again. One of the first things he saw was that Orfik was playing with the young ones, and that Ivalu was always with them.

Chapter Seven

WHEN brothers are together they have a natural union against any opposing force. If one of them needs help, he has it without having to go for outside aid. If his meat gives out he does not have to be grateful for being fed by a stranger. And now that Mitzerk was married, his two brothers, Tatiak and Apilak, were a pleasure to him because they helped him in many things in which he, as a younger man, lacked practice.

All three of them loved singing, although their voices were coarse and hard and it was difficult for their wives to get used to their endless songs. For they sang not only in the winter when people would have enjoyed it as amusement in the long darkness but also in the summer. Often the three of them would go into one of their tents, fasten sealskins over the gut windows so that it would be dark and their laziness would not be so easily seen, and then the song would roll out of their throats. They would stand facing each other for a long time, beating on drums and bending the upper part of their bodies in a dance. And then they would whirl so fast that their faces could not be clearly seen, working themselves into a frenzy, twisting and squirming, letting the drums boom while they sang and sang. Ivalu often wished she could go out and play with her friends, or just go to sleep, as she was tired at the end of the long day.

The wives of Tatiak and Apilak were older than she and more experienced in family life. She had seen the scar on the leg of Apilak's wife, and knew it had come from a fight she and Apilak had had, in which he stabbed her with a knife. From Tatiak's tent there often came the sound of a woman's screams, when Tatiak was beating *his* wife. Both brothers were quick-tempered and lost control when their wives talked back to them.

The three brothers decided to travel to a nearby sea to catch salmon. Ivalu went along and was very bored, although it was nice when they caught a lot of salmon or rabbits. But it was uncomfortable to sleep under the open sky, and one day, when it was raining, she asked permission to go home. At this they all laughed at her, and her face got hot. She cried and said she was freezing in the dampness. Her sisters-in-law laughed and said: "Here is a young married woman whose grandmother kept her all wrapped up. When she was finally let out into the air she was soft, and never hardened into a human being!"

It was not very easy for her, as she had no one to advise or help her. One day, while she was patching one of her husband's boots and was trying to cut off the thread, she cut a hole in the boot. Everything always seemd to go wrong for her and she was glad when they got home.

On her arrival she went right to her grandmother's tent and told her all about their trip. Time went by quickly and she forgot completely that she should be at home cooking dinner for her husband. Suddenly his voice was outside the tent, loud and angry: "Ivalu. Ivalu. Come back from your visit!"

She was being called home, as often happened when she stayed away too long. Her grandmother looked at her and said, "Hurry!" She sounded so sharp that Ivalu knew Ama did not feel sorry for her. She thought: "Grandmother is getting old and no longer realizes that I would rather be here with her."

Another time she came home and the brothers were sitting with their wives. She was carrying a pair of her husband's boots which her grandmother had fixed and soled.

"Ak! I am envious," Apilak's wife said. "It must be a happy woman who can take her sewing to someone else to do, and so does not have to hurt her fingers with a needle."

"Yes," Tatiak's wife said, mockingly. "I wish my husband had a wife who sewed as well as Ivalu."

They kept on amusing themselves at her expense, and said that, since she was a young married woman who did not sew well, it was wise for her to take her

work to her grandmother: "And, as your grandmother also has many skins, you can get your material at the same time."

For the first time Mitzerk got really angry at his
wife. He jumped from the bed and tore the boots
from Ivalu's hand.

"As if one didn't have plenty of skins!" he
shouted. "Is one to be dressed from the catch of a
stranger, as if one had no hands and could not hunt
for one's self? Why do you bring other people's
things into my tent?"

He took his knife, cut the boots into strips and
flung them into her face. Ivalu was being punished in
front of others.

The ice had broken up and the men went out in
their *kayaks*. The brothers would go out with the
other trappers, and would often stay away a while,
waiting in the foothills for the herds of walrus which
would pass there. If the winds blew up, they were
forced to stay on the other side of the land for several
days before they could return home. On these days
it was the women who were heard. For, when women
are alone, they talk as if they had no masters, and
forget the things they have been taught about custom
and form.

Few of the men remained in the settlement but
among these was Orfik. As he had no wife, he would
come to Mitzerk's tent and ask Ivalu to mend his

things. He brought her stocking skins that were to be sewn, and she chewed them when she went visiting. The other women saw that Ivalu, without permission from her husband, was chewing skins for a stranger.

When the trappers returned they laughed about their experiences.

"There we were, wet and freezing, with no clothes to change, although our women had plenty of things just on the other side of the fjord."

When Mitzerk saw that new stockings were hanging in his tent, he lost his good humor and became angry. A young husband is very particular about following customs. After he had gone to sleep Ivalu noticed that the stockings were gone from the tent pole. She saw them sticking out from beneath Mitzerk's head. The next morning he put the stockings on.

"Ak! joy is in this house. My little wife has unexpectedly made me new clothes." And he purposely let the stocking bands show over the top of his boots, so that everyone could see that for his shame he got satisfaction.

A few days later the trappers again went to sea. This time Orfik went along. He killed one seal and then trailing his catch behind his boat, started to paddle homewards as though the hunt were over. The others called after him, and Mitzerk knew of whom he was thinking. But Mitzerk was young and did not want to make himself ridiculous by paddling after Orfik to guard his wife. That evening cries were heard from Ivalu's tent.

"So some of the trappers paddled home . . ." Mitzerk shouted, and beat her.

Ivalu lost her temper and said that she had not asked any one to come back, and that she could not help it if some came back and others stayed out.

Later they all ate together and one could notice that each time Mitzerk wiped his fingers he did so on a fur rag which he tore from the upper end of his stocking. While they were still eating, Ivalu came running up. She hurried by with her head turned away and disappeared into her grandmother's tent. Old Merquzaq, who sat among the other men, laughed a little:

"It is sad, when people stop beating their wives. If one can't get angry, one loses much joy."

No more was said. None of the men wanted to appear to show any interest in a miserable woman, and after they had eaten, they all went to their own tents.

"One has become sleepy and goes to rest," Mitzerk called in front of Merquzaq's tent. He stood waiting to see if there was any answer or if Ivalu would come out. But his young wife remained at her grandparents' and he had to sleep alone.

When the others woke up, Mitzerk had already gone out hunting. He stayed away until late that night, and when he returned he brought a reindeer he had shot. It happened so seldom in the settlement that one got reindeer meat to eat, and it was such a delicacy, that Ivalu forgot her anger and went home to her husband.

The hide was beautiful and all the women admired it. Its possession gave Ivalu a new sense of importance, and she told her friends she was surprised they had not already lighted a blubber fire.

"One has decided to cook a little meat," she said. "Hang the pot over the fire, but first throw out the old soup."

Hurriedly some of the women took the pot of soup, which had gotten thick from cooking and recooking, and threw it to the dogs, who lapped it all up and licked the pot clean.

"One needs water," she said then, "fresh water from the river." They hurried to bring the water and light the fire, and, when this had been done Mitzerk brought over the meat.

The two young people felt very pleased at being able, for the first time, to invite their neighbors for a special feast. Some of the older women, especially, were pleased, and said that at last one felt satisfaction in the mouthcorners. Mitzerk saved some of the meat, and threw it in his tent. Nobody missed seeing that this included the tongue, and some of the old women laughed to themselves, remembering when they were young and their husbands brought reindeer tongue home to them.

When the meat was cooked, Ivalu served it. Her husband had made the catch and now she could do the talking.

"Ak! what one offers is not really tasty," she said, "but please eat it to make me happy."

"She speaks the truth," Mitzerk said, enjoying his triumph. "I am a miserable dunce who does not know how to catch anything which one would wish to eat."

Orfik had built himself a small house, and Mitzerk took a reindeer leg and took it to the home of his rival.

"Perhaps you might like reindeer meat," he said. "I have nothing else to offer." He came back later and threw the unmarried man a bundle of ligaments from the reindeer's back. "Ak! perhaps your wife needs threads," he said, grinning.

The summer passed. The three men caught meat for the house, and even Orfik was diligent and had stores laid by for the winter.

"When the ice comes," he said, "I am thinking of making a trip. So one needs a few supplies."

And then, one day, Mitzerk, Apilak and Orfik went out hunting together. Before they had gone far, Apilak shouted that there was water coming into his *kayak*, and he was getting wet.

"One turns back and fixes it," he shouted to them.

The others went on. They were away all day, and the next morning—only one of them came back. It was Orfik. He was towing Mitzerk's *kayak*, but it was empty. Fear gripped the settlement. Death had also been out hunting, and had caught one of these two. Orfik sat out in his *kayak* and looked sadly in front of him, and the settlement knew that the three brothers were now only two.

Ivalu was silent as the *kayak* of her husband was drawn up on the land, but, when they all looked at her, whispering to each other, she rushed into her tent and they could hear her sobbing.

Orfik put away his weapons, then sat and told Merquzaq what had happened. They had harpooned a walrus, but the bladder float on Mitzerk's line slid around so that the line was pulled tight across the *kayak* instead of away from it. Mitzerk was caught, and the animal's struggles pulled him over. Then the walrus attacked, and pulled him under water with him.

"Ak! the capable Mitzerk whose meat we ate so often," said the women, who sat indoors and mourned.

The settlement was quiet. No one went catching

and there was no loud talk among the people. Two days later the children, who were running around and playing, saw Orfik go into Ivalu's tent. But then they heard Ivalu talking angrily, and shortly Orfik came out. Apilak, Mitzerk's brother, stopped him.

"Recently a *kayak* was towed back to the settlement and one noticed your lance was missing!"

"It remained stuck in the walrus, after I hurled it to defend my catching partner," Orfik said.

When he came to the fire to eat, everyone drew away from him. When he handed a piece of meat from which he had taken a bite to a small boy, the youngster threw it to the dogs. Tatiak then asked what the killed man had said as he sank, since he must have had ample time to talk. But Orfik only sat silent, looking down in front of him.

"I will not speak," he said, and the whole settlement knew that Orfik was keeping something to himself.

Shortly thereafter Ivalu took her pelts, rolled them up, and carried the bundle to her grandmother's tent.

"Let me sleep here, where there are others," she said. "If one cannot be alone, it is best to be with relatives."

The mourning brothers planned to say something to Orfik the next day at meal time. Orfik had changed greatly. His face looked strained, and he kept an axe next to him, as though he feared an attack and wanted to be prepared. Everyone looked at him while he ate, and nobody talked. Afterwards, when he left the group, the children all ran after him and looked at him as though he were a stranger who had just arrived.

"Why did you not speak?" Tatiak asked Apilak, when they were alone.

"Am I the oldest?" Apilak wanted to know. "Be patient. Words will be spoken when the right time comes!"

But the time never came, because the next morning Orfik hung by a cord from the meat rack of the settlement, and was dead.

Among the settlers there was a man who was a cousin of Orfik's, and even he said that he did not grieve over this second man to die. Nothing else was said about Orfik, who hanged himself out of fear because the people looked at him with suspicion.

Ivalu was once more a little girl. She played on the beach and threw stones into the water. Every once in a while, however, her brothers-in-law reminded her of the stores of meat which she had in the hills, and told her she should divide it with them. But as far as she was concerned they were like strangers. They had already taken their brother's *kayak*, and used his tent to patch their own.

One late summer day the body of Mitzerk was found. Only the hair, an arm and part of the back were left—everything else had been torn by eels. Ivalu cried bitterly as she thought of her husband, young and laughing, and now eaten by tiny animals. His brothers examined the body carefully and looked for marks. But everything was in shreds and it was impossible to see whether there had been a lance thrust.

"One is without knowledge of what happened," Tatiak said. "Now only a burial for our brother is necessary."

They buried him on the hill and laid big stones over his body. When Ivalu went to the grave, she saw that the brothers had killed none of his dogs nor buried his weapons, as was the custom. They had divided them among themselves.

Soon it was autumn, and fox trapping began. Ivalu was a clever trapper and made many trips with her grandmother to set traps. She wanted to catch enough animals to make a new fur coat for herself.

They decided she should travel South, to forget her sorrow. Her mother and Uvdluriak lived on the middle fjords. There she was to remain, and not return to the lee side until her thoughts had again become happy.

Chapter Eight

AUTUMN came. The air was cold and quiet, and ice covered the fjords.

Ivalu kept more and more away from the men of the settlement, in her grandfather's tent. She continually asked him to tell her stories about white men, and particularly those whom he had seen and known.

Most of all, Ivalu liked to hear about the great Peary. The first time he came he took six people home with him. They now lived in the land of the white men and ate their food, without even working for it.

When the new ice was thick enough Merquzaq moved to the South, taking Ama and Ivalu with him. They went to Umanak, where her step-father, Uvdluriak, and her mother, Kazaluk, still lived. They now had several more children and Uvdluriak did the thinking for the settlement.

Ivalu had come as a widow so she went very slowly from the sled to the house. Her mother and the children stood before the entrance and waited silently. Ivalu went in, sat down on the bed, and remained there with her head bowed and wtihout speaking.

Old Merquzaq was busy tying up his dogs and unloading the sleds. Only after all this had been done did he go inside and join the others. The deep silence still prevailed. But Merquzaq, who was the oldest member of the family, was quiet for only a short time. When he decided that the silence had lasted long enough, he said, "Herewith one comes to visit, but not with as large a following as one could have brought last year. Therefore one's thoughts are filled with sorrow."

Uvdluriak said that one had heard of the event, and Kazaluk said "Oh, ja ja!", and so they decided to eat immediately. "We are alive," Uvdluriak said, "and much meat comes into our house. It should be eaten, so that it does not become too much."

Later, Ivalu visited the other houses, and was happy to be able to play with her little half sisters.

But one day a new adventure came to her.

A shout came from the darkness out over the ice: "Minik has returned! The great Minik comes to visit!" And quickly the men ran out of the houses and stood by the meat scaffold, and the women put on their fur coats, climbed on top of the house passages, and stared out into the darkness.

They were sleds from Cape York, led by the great Mayark and his dogs, who came whirling up noisily as was his habit when visiting. Among his followers was Minik, the son of Krizuk. They had not seen Minik since he was a child. Now he had become like a white man and had the talk of the white men, and spoke so that the people could not understand him.

Mayark said that last summer Minik had been brought to Cape York by a whale catcher and put on the land there with very few possessions. He moved in with Mayark. He had learned to talk a little, and to drive a team and paddle a *kayak*. He was clumsy at both, although he was a young man and as strong as the best trappers of the tribe.

They didn't remember Minik. They did remember how they had feared for Krizuk, Minik's father, when he went on his journey to the land of the white men. Evidently their fears were justified, for all the grown-ups who had gone to the white men's land, had died of longing for their native food. Only Minik lived, but without happiness in this strange country, and for years he had begged to be allowed to return home. Now, at last, he had been brought back on a ship, but without the many presents one would have expected.

Merquzaq said that Minik had certainly done nothing to distinguish himself. But he was big and strong and laughed a great deal, so everybody asked him to visit them, and when he did, they served their best food to this unusual guest.

They talked about Minik's father and his companions, who were now dead in the land of the white men. Ivalu was unhappy that she couldn't ask Minik about all the unusual things he had seen. She was burning to know why he had left a place where there were so many bright colors, and mirrors, and sugar, and other good-tasting things. But she was only a miserable woman and could have no words for a man.

After she had lived with her grandmother for a while, they talked about its being a good thing to marry her off. Minik heard that she was not promised to any other man, so it was decided that next year he would marry her, and they would settle down here with the others. Ivalu listened to all this, but she had no desire for him. She decided one thing, however: if she married him, she would learn the white men's talk and a great deal about them from him!

From time to time one would get from the ships the thin white skins which the white men called "paper" and on which were pictures of the white men's land. The ones she liked best were the pictures of those who, judging from their faces and figures, were the women. They were always wrapped in long pieces of things to show their wealth by their clothes. One couldn't see their pants. She wondered if they didn't wear any or if they wanted to hide them and just show how much material they had to make jackets and pants from.

One day when Ivalu was alone in the house, Minik came in. He started to smile, and talked in his peculiar manner. She remembered that although Peary talked the language like a child, one could understand him, but she could not understand Minik. She was also embarrassed at being alone with the man she was going to marry and about whom she knew nothing. He sat quietly for a while, and then suddenly spoke again but she still did not understand him. Then he jumped swiftly to her and put his arms around her neck. Ak! men are always so impulsive and want a woman all the time! But a woman who is attacked defends herself with all her strength. He had pushed her over on her back and now she tried to force him away from her with her hands, and strained her body to get free. Minik became more eager, and pulled her head to him, and acted the way she had heard women say all white men acted. He was pressing his face against hers and trying to make their mouths touch. She was so surprised at this peculiar desire that she permitted it calmly. He rubbed his mouth against hers and then he loosened his hold on her slightly. Then, as the children came running into the house, he jumped on the side bed plank and Ivalu got up. She thought that perhaps he had wanted to kiss her, but in his lust had been too confused to rub his nose against hers.

Not long after this occurrence Minik and Mayark went further north to visit other settlements. The morning they left, Ivalu stood there and watched them disappear behind the icebergs. She felt that life held no happiness for her at all.

IVALU • THE ESKIMO WIFE

Through the winter she stayed with her mother
and her clothes began to wear out. She herself did
not go trapping, and the skins which Uvdluriak
brought home were used partly for the children's
clothes and partly for furs for her mother.

A good part of the fox skins were set aside by Uvdluriak for himself. He wanted to buy a rifle in the
spring, when the ships came back. He wanted to
own a lot of rifles so that, when one of the young
men wanted to borrow a gun, he could say, "Ak!
which gun shall I give you? Which one should I
choose? I really don't know which gun is best suited
to you." Then he could laugh, because he would
have shown himself to be a rich man able to refer
to many belongings which the others could not buy
for themselves.

One of the little boys first saw the ship far out
between the islands.

A ship at this season could not be a whaler, for
they were at Cape York, as usual at this time of year.
Uvdluriak and Merquzaq had seen them there. They
themselves had travelled the long road over the glacier with their winter catch, which the whale catchers
valued so highly. They had come back with two guns
and with much of the white men's food, which the
people so enjoyed.

They hoped that this was a ship that would be

more interesting to them than another whaler. Someone said it must be Peary returning, although last
year he had said his visits were over and, until now,
his word had always been reliable.

That was why the arrival of this ship was important. Perhaps they were new people, who wanted to
make marks on paper about the country. But, no
matter who this was, they were happy, because ships
always brought joy.

Ivalu stood behind the row of women and thought
excitedly. Whenever white men were talked about
she was always filled with a longing for something
she could not understand. Now they were coming
to her— The ship was coming nearer. At first it
looked like a small ice bear with a mast pointing in
the air, but now it was taking on the form of ship.
One could hear its thunder as it was driven through
the water by its tail fin.

The white men did not steer straight toward the
houses, but sailed into a little inlet on the other side
of the point.

"They want protection from the waves, to save
their ship," an old woman said. Ivalu felt jealous that
an old woman knew so much about the white men,
and was right about what she had said.

The ship was close now and the white men could
be seen running back and forth on the deck. Some
moved about while others stood still. These were the

leaders, who were telling the others what to do. It was a sight they did not get tired of watching. Only the children, who could not keep their minds on one thing very long, started to play again. They did not understand the pleasures which came with the white men's visits.

Suddenly there was a loud noise from the ship, which frightened them, but then they saw it was the huge iron hook which came from the prow and splashed into the water. An enormous iron rope followed it with a loud clanking. It was the anchor, which bit into the bottom and prevented the ship from drifting away.

Now that the ship no longer moved, the men in the *kayaks* went closer. A ladder was let down over the side and one after another, the men climbed from the *kayaks* aboard ship, stood there, and laughed at the white men. They could see, now, that the ship was smaller than was usual. There were not as many men on board and all the faces were unfamiliar. One of the men was dressed in white, the distinguishing clothes of the cook. One knew he was not the master of the ship, but he was always the friendliest, so they crowded around him and his little house from which came the smells of good-tasting dishes.

Suddenly a man stepped forward and spoke in a loud voice. He laughed a lot and looked friendly, and he kept repeating something which he evidently was trying to make them understand. He kept at them so earnestly that some of them stopped thinking about the cook and food, and began to listen to him. They said something, themselves, and finally it became clear that he could talk their language. At this they were very pleased and told one another that they understood the stranger.

Then the white man came up to one of them, took his hand, and pulled it as though he wanted the man to come to him. But, when the man started to follow him, the stranger let go and went to another one of them, and pulled a little on his right hand, too. He acted in this peculiar manner until he had pulled a little on everyone's right hand.

A man who looked like one of the people stepped forward. He began to talk and it was clear that he was a man like themselves, and that his tongue had become frail from eating the white man's food for so many years, so that he could not speak words correctly.

A white man, whom his companions called Bangé, had the same habit as all white men, that of telling their names and wanting to know the names of all the people they meet. He had not learned enough of the language or customs of the people to know shame.

"My name is Bangé. What is your name?" he asked Uvdluriak, who laughed and said he did not know.

"Don't you know your own name?" Bangé asked. He believed Uvdluriak really did not know his own name.

"Others will tell my name," Uvdluriak said. "One does not remember one's own."

Some of the others answered immediately that his name was Uvdluriak. Another man came forward, and said his name was Karl Boezen. But that name was difficult to say, so most people called him "Bozi," and that did just as well.

The men of the ship pulled some cables and a small boat that hung on the back of the ship was lowered into the water. Bangé, Bozi and several others got in it. A man whom they called Elias was asked if he wanted to come along, but he shook his head. The others rowed to shore. There the women stood lined up in two rows. They kept their eyes away from the white men and looked only at the children, who were playing. The little boys seemed especially amusing to them and, when one of them fell, they all laughed a lot. Now and then they threw a stolen glance at the boat from which the white men were getting out. The men were so tall that it made the young women shudder. When they noticed the men looking at them, the women looked quickly away. They looked back to the little boys, cried out to one another, and laughed some more. No one should be able to travel away and say that the women of

Umanak had stood in lines and been too interested and happy over strange white sailors.

But the men went straight toward them. A white man never knows shame. He neither cares to save a woman from embarrassment nor is he ashamed to openly pay attention to miserable women. The one who walked in the lead and had a big nose, started to talk to them. He said that he had wanted to come here for a long time. Maybe the stupid man thought that the women would answer him, for he paused. But it was old Merquzaq who answered, by right of being the oldest and their equal. He said, "The white man is to be pitied in his long desire to visit this miserable place. Of all lands this is the worst, and it is occupied by a miserable people who live in wretched hovels and have not enough to eat. The only wise thing for the white man to do is to return to the ship as quickly as possible and sail away from here."

The women stood looking down in front of them, and they noticed that the white man's boots were different from any they had ever seen. This amused them, but they did not show it. They took good care that no one could say, either, that they had thrown amused glances at the strangers.

The one who had talked again pulled Uvdluriak and Torngé by the hands and then he walked up the beach with them. His companions followed, but the people stayed where they were, gathered around the boat, which was drawn up on the beach and had two oarsmen in it. It was obvious that these two were not big men among the white men, and were just helpers who had no thoughts of their own. In front of men like these there was no reason to be ashamed and when the children, in their young eagerness, had gone nearer the boat, all the rest crowded closer, also. The oarsmen began to say wonderful words and to laugh and the people answered, although they knew they were not understood. They laughed a lot and the helpers put their hands into pouches which were sewn into their clothes, and pulled out tobacco in thin rolls which were covered with paper. These they put into the hands of the women and young men, and took fire out of their boxes and lighted the tobacco. Ivalu was given one of these rolls and it tasted as if all her longing for the white men were gathered into smoke.

Further down the beach one could see the white man with the big nose seat himself on a rock, while Uvdluriak and Torngé stood in front of him. They spoke eagerly. Shortly afterwards, they returned to the women and Uvdluriak told them that the white man was a great thinker, whose thoughts decided for all on board the ship and should also decide for all those here. He said that the white man was also born in this land, but on the coast, further to the side, where the people talked with a crooked tongue but used the same words.

Everyone was staring at the strange men, and one of the women whispered that perhaps where the man came from the biggest nose was important, for this man, who thought for all, had the biggest nose one had ever seen. And one could see from his mouth that he was used to commanding, and that he always had wise words in his head, before which one had to bow.

The thinker told them that a house had to be built, as a white man was going to live among them. One of the men came and said that they had made a mistake and anchored the ship in the wrong place. The houses lay on the other side of the point, and it was better to live there, since there one had a view over the fjords and could see the tracks of animals to better advantage.

The thinker laughed a little and said that his ship must lie where the wind coud do it no harm, and that ice is not bad and that was where his house should stand. He decided to build close to the river so that the bringing of water should be less difficult. By this thought he showed the people that he forgot nothing. He said also that the house should stand on solid rock, and not on the ground, which became soft in the summer. As he at last made his decision, he

said to all the people that he wished help in bringing
his many possessions ashore:

"It is clear that itw ill be an effort for you, but
I would like to see how industrious you are and how
quickly you can do this. That way I can learn whether
you are suited to extraordinary work."

They all promised that they would help, and the
white men got into their boat and rowed back to the
ship. Uvdluriak and Torngé went with them, but
the rest stayed on the shore talking of all they had
seen, and of the remarkable man and of the experience
that this day had brought to their settlement.

Only now did they realize that a white man
wanted to live among them. They could not hold
back their joy, and they laughed and shouted so
that the mountains could hear it, and the whole world
around them could hear it, too.

Some oarsmen rowed over and nodded to the
people to come aboard. Ivalu had such a desire to go
that she said to the woman next to her "Come, let
us go! Surely he wishes us all to come!"

But now all the women turned against her, ignor-
ing her and saying to each other: "Ak! listen to the
talk of a woman! She surely is one who wants to go
on a ship by herself, she who has no man to say what
she should do."

This talk made her so unhappy that her face became hot right down to her neck. She knew she was

about to cry so she turned, shouted an angry word, and ran to her tent. She undressed and laid down to sleep, unhappily feeling that she did not want to show herself again until the ship had sailed away. She wanted to stay right there in the tent until there was ice, and she could travel north to a place where it was possible to live without being bothered by white men.

The thinker opened the ship and showed the people how to lift the cases and put them into the boat. A few tents were put up, which the thinker said would be living quarters for the white men until the house was finished. They were small tents, made of a thin, white skin which had not been taken from an animal. Ak! it was so pretty, this white in the summer! It made one think of snow and the joy of the winters. Yes, when white men came they always brought pretty and pleasant things.

A huge pile of wood was brought to shore. Ak! how the wood gushed forth from the big ship! It was not nearly so big as Peary's, but, remarkably, it had more in its insides. The women saw how the wood, piece by piece, was brought to shore by the boat, and it went on and on. They kept saying, "Now, surely, no more wood can come! The land of the white men must have been stripped bare, and their reserve exhausted!" But it continued—always more and more wood.

Now the thinker came on shore and shouted to the women that he wanted to talk to them. They were glad, and understood that his thoughts included them, too. It happened that he wanted them to help with the work! He said that every woman should bend over, take a piece of wood on her shoulder, and carry it to the place where the house was to stand. They all stood still, and were ashamed. A white man had surely spoken remarkable words! And he said again, "I want you to help with the work."

They thought that, perhaps, he wished to joke and say things which provoked laughter, so they tried to laugh a little. But a few words from him quickly showed that he indeed had the remarkable thought that a woman should carry heavy objects. They were glad when Merquzaq stepped up and said it was against the wisdom of the ancients for women to occupy themselves with things which were the privileges of men. He said that the great thinker was in a land where the duties of women were to sew and bear children and to help men on the hunt. But men did not want their women to do things which were bad for their clothes, made their walk heavy, and tired them out too much for love in the night.

At that the white man laughed, and took back his request. Merquzaq said, "I am too old to win the favor of women. However, all the young men will carry heavy loads, if the women are watching; for all men like to distinguish themselves to arouse the admiration of miserable women."

The great thinker knew that he had come to a land where the customs were different from his own, and he said Merquzaq was right.

Toward evening work was stopped and the thinker brought many kinds of food ashore. Over a mighty fire a huge pot of tea was cooked, and so many cups were used that every two or three people had one cup all to themselves. Everybody was filled with good-tasting things.

Ivalu was not there. When she heard later about all the delicious things they had eaten, she said she was glad she had not been present. She did not want to eat the white men's food; she wanted to go away, and only wished that soon there would be ice.

Next morning the thinker awoke before anyone else. He had a box with which he made loud noises to waken the people so that work should start. They were all still sleepy, since the bringing ashore of the possessions yesterday had tired them out, and they had stayed up until late in the night and talked about the remarkable things which they had seen. So they did not care about the box, and slept on. But shortly they were again awakened by the man himself, who came to their tents, opened the flaps, and called laughingly in to them, "Ak! I have come to a people

IVALU • THE ESKIMO WIFE

who are all big sleepers. Maybe it is better to wait
a few days, until you all wake up again."

The people of the settlement, who did not know
about being awakened when they wished to sleep,
laughed at this remarkable behavior, and then began
to dress. The thinker had brought Elias and Bozi
with him. The three of them walked among the
tents together. The women were most interested in
Elias, but he was shy and only answered when his
master spoke to him.

When all the people had been awakened they were
told the day would start with a common meal. They
hurried to where the white men's tents were pitched
and found that food was ready, and steam coming
from the great kettle was a sign that tea was being
cooked. Oarsmen came from the ship and brought
more good things ashore, and the thinker cried that
the ship would not like to sail away with the thought
that the people here were too sleepy to do anything.
Then he laughed heartily, and they were ashamed.
They decided to work with full strength to make up
for the time missed by sleeping too long.

When the boat was rowed back to the ship, Elias
went along. When the master noticed this he called
him, but Elias acted as though he did not hear. He
leaped on the ship, and one saw him run into one of
the little houses on board.

The thinker also went out to the ship, and

Uvdluriak went with him. Later, when Uvdluriak returned, he told the people that the master explained to him what took place, as the two white men spoke in their own language, which he could not understand.

When Uvdluriak and the thinker got up on the boat, they found Elias in tears. Uvdluriak got great sympathy for Elias, because he was so unhappy that he cried and acted like a woman. Elias said he was afraid of all the men here. He had a spirit in his own land whom he called "God," who was not here, and he was afraid because the people wore long hair, had enormous knives, and spoke strange words.

Then the white man spoke to Elias and said that it was according to his own will that he had come to live here, and that, after all, his situation at home had been very sad. It was he who had wanted to go away, until the happenings which made him leave had been forgotten. At this Elias said yes, but he had expected to travel to a country where there was nothing to fear, and where people were like himself. Only now did Uvdluriak notice that Elias' hair was cut. Perhaps it was a sign of ugliness in the South to leave one's hair long, although one only did it to keep one's ears warm in the winter. Therefore he laughed, but Elias got angry and said, "You see? Here is a man who laughs at my misfortune! It is clear they are not good people, and that is why I am afraid."

Uvdluriak, when the thinker turned and told him
what Elias had said, hastened to say he did not laugh
out of bad will. He had only laughed because of the
strange things Elias had said, and because he could
see that Elias came from a foreign land where there
are no customs and manners.

Now the white man told Elias that he should be
without fear, especially as it was good for him to be
with other people. Elias shouted that he knew he
was hated, because he had stepped beyond the laws
in his own country.

Later Uvdluriak asked what rules had been stepped
beyond, and the great thinker told him that white
men had a rule that one can not take the possessions
of others, and other laws as to how one should behave
toward women. There existed all sorts of laws to ease
the lives of the people who are not masters in the
land. And Uvdluriak told all this to the people, who
agreed that Elias must be nobler than the others, if
he could step beyond the rules of the white men and
mock their laws. Perhaps he should have been respected more than he had been so far. Possibly the
cause of his ill humor was that the people had not
immediately noticed his greatness. But now they
decided to make good for this in every way.

When, around evening, Elias rowed ashore with
the white men, Uvdluriak went to him and told him
that the settlement was very happy that he had come.

Elias said little, but his anger seemed a little appeased. For a long time Elias was treated as the one deserving of the most respect, because he had taken things belonging to other people and had shown himself as one having no fear of the white men's law.

A few days of hard work followed, but whenever it came time to eat, there was a feast. They ate in the morning as well as in the middle of the day and at night. Then there was no more wood to be taken ashore, but one morning the big thinker came and said that now they could show how able the people really were. He said he was very pleased at what had been done so far, but now a few black stones had to be brought ashore. He said these would dirty the bearskin trousers of the people, and that those who were not very capable and did not wish to win his gratitude could decline to help in this work. Several of the men laughed and said they were well travelled people and knew all about these black stones, which could burn. They had seen them thrown into the enormous fireplaces on ships

"We will take your burning stones and bring them ashore. We are people who are always dirty. We live in a land of filth. What you are telling us about is nothing compared with what we are used to."

They were all given thin trousers made of dark material, which they pulled over their pants, so it was fun to carry the stones ashore and put them in a huge pile.

One evening all the white men from the ship came ashore and one of them brought along a box which could be pulled out and made long and pushed together and made very short. At the same time it pushed out a lot of peculiar noises at which the white men seemed to feel pleasure. Merquzaq said that he had seen the same thing on Peary's ship. It was necessary not to let the white men see how laughable they made themselves with this spectacle, because they often got angry at this. One of the men held a stick and rubbed it across sinew threads, which were stretched lengthwise on a box which he held under his chin. This produced noises which reminded one of a bird mountain. They felt sorry for the sailors, who must lack entertainment to be satisfied with such poor amusement. The white men sat there and their eyes looked as though they had eaten too much. Such were their minds as they listened to those screaming noises.

That night there was much to eat. They served tea and coffee, little pieces of bread with sugar on them, and tobacco in little sticks as well as in pipes. The great thinker stood up on a box and began to talk quite a lot, at first in his own language, and all the white men listened. Then he began to talk in the people's way and said he wanted to build a house where one could get necessary things. And he said he had found better people than he had expected. After this, however, his speech became very complicated and drawn out, so that the people forgot to listen. They wondered why he continued to talk without caring what his listeners had to answer. When he stepped down the white men burst into loud shouts and took off their caps and waved them over their heads.

After this another white man got up on the box and spoke in his own tongue and, when he finished, his countrymen again lifted their caps and burst into peculiar shouts. The people understood that these were the same words they had used before, and there were sometimes high notes and sometimes low ones, in the shouts. They remained completely serious and, when it was over, the great man said it was a song from their country. The people tried not to laugh at them.

After the meal, they went around and looked over the different possessions, which lay there. The young white men went again to the women and spoke to them direct. But not one of them, evidently, really had the desire to acquire a wife, even for the time he was there, or he would have turned to her husband and asked him for the right to borrow her. Some of them tried to pull the women for a little distance up on the hill, but they always slipped away and ran off. The children and all the others laughed very much at this. From this one began to believe that the white men desired only their own women, and were not like Peary's men, who were always ready to borrow women, even secretly, for Peary had forbidden it.

A few days later it was decided that the ship should sail away. The people were greatly disappointed, because the one who was thinking for all the white men would have been the best one to make decisions for the whole settlement; yes, even for all peoples. They spoke sadly of his intention to leave with the ship and leave Bozi and Elias in the settlement.

The thinker explained he belonged to those who always return to a place once they had been there. They might, then, expect his visit at any time. He might come by sled or he might come back with the ship. But always his thoughts would follow them, and, when he came back he would overcome some of their wants with certain remedies of the white men.

The next day the ship left. But before it did, there was a strange scene. Elias cried on the ship, before he came ashore. Into the face of the thinker came a hard expression, which they had never seen before. He grabbed Elias' arm and evidently said harsh words which had to be obeyed. Elias sat in the boat and cried like a little child that is freezing. The people were all so surprised at this that they forgot to look after the ship until it was far out, hurrying to its own land.

The women stood there in rows and looked after it as they had done when it came. And to the men it seemed as though the land had changed because a white man had come among them.

Chapter Nine

IVALU should have been filled with fear over the uncertainty of her future. Sometimes a woman got a man who was an able provider, but she also ran the danger that he would be without luck in his hunting and trapping. Ivalu, however, did not occupy herself with this thought for very long. Instead she ran and played, for it was amusing to jump around among the cases which were piled on the beach. When she tumbled over the piles of lumber they rolled and slid like calving icebergs.

Suddenly, in the midst of her play, she noticed that a white man was looking at her. Her face became quite hot, because he faced her directly and stared at her. He called to her, so she had to look away. She was aware of the same feeling she had had as a child on Peary's ship. Then, too, she had been afraid of the white men, although everyone told her there was no cause for fear.

The white man came up to her and held his hand out in front of his body, as he always did in greeting. There was a smile around his mouth and she saw that his eyes were different from the eyes of the people. The part that was usually black looked like the sky without clouds, and, in her astonishment at this, she forgot she was a woman facing a strange

man, and she kept looking up at him. His smile was
so friendly that she smiled, too.

"What is your name?" he asked.

She looked away and said she did not know. The
white man was puzzled, and asked again, "Come,
now, what is your name?"

Ivalu said that someone else must tell him her
name, that she did not know what it was. A few
boys, passing by, told him her name was Ivalu. This
embarrassed her and she ran home quickly, telling
her mother she wished she lived in a settlement where
there were no ships and no white men.

The white man's name was Bozi. He had such
remarkably bad manners that he went to everybody,
pointed to himself, and said, "My name is Bozi!",
and then asked everybody what *their* names were.

But he did not care what people thought of him.
Elias managed to tell them that Bozi lived in a land
even further away than Peary's but, even so, he
had managed to learn something of the people's language. In his land it was not considered enough to be
able to talk only to those around one, as the white
men often sought contact with inhabitants of distant
lands.

Day after day the people heard the ringing of
Bozi's hammer as the white man worked to build
himself a house. He did not want to build it out of
stones and sod, like the people, but wanted to show

his wealth of wood and therefore built it out of that. He had big pouches of nails which he drove into the wood, and the house grew and was very large. It was strange—white men had houses full of little houses, which they called "rooms." First one came into a small room, turned right into another room and then further into a third one. And in the center was still another room, in which Bozi only slept. In the front room of the house was a square iron box for cooking, on the top of which were round holes covered with rings which one could make larger or smaller to fit the size of the pots. Bozi had immeasureable quantities of cooking utensils.

When the house was finished, he sent Elias to all the tents to tell the people that visits were expected and that later they were all to come there and eat. But not one of them wanted to wait. The children all ran over, shouting that they wanted to be the first, and the grown-ups got together to decide what to do. Merquzaq said it was true they were asked to come later on, but the reason might be that the white man had to cook the food. If this were so, it might be interesting to go and watch his preparations. Everybody thought he was right, and immediately they all went over. The men went first, the women following, staying together so as not to seem too anxious and to preserve their dignity. Each one took along an auk skin, which she chewed to make an undershirt for her husband.

When they arrived at Bozi's house, he was standing by the pot. He turned around and laughed. "Wait a bit! Wait a bit!" he said, but they all crowded through the door and stood around to see what he was doing. Elias explained that Bozi wanted to express his gladness over having gotten a house in the settlement, and this time they were all to eat white men's food. He had not yet had time to go trapping and get meat for himself, but later he was going out with the others to catch. He had already told them that in his many cases were articles waiting only for their fox pelts. Uvdluriak was the man who spoke for the entire settlement, and now he told Bozi he had made his journey in vain.

"For we have seen the things you have brought with you and they are valuable, but our pelts are always miserable. Our skins are completely useless, and under no circumstances would we be so presumptuous as to compare them with your precious things."

Bozi opened a huge case out of which he took a large number of little pots with tight-fitting covers. He opened them with a knife and poured their contents into a big kettle. It was something which had already been cooked in the land of the white men.

The women looked longingly at the little pots, which were good for carrying water. They would also be useful to the catchers who went out in kayaks and wanted to cook on the way. Ivalu thought, "If I had some pots like those, I would take a long trip along the coast, and stay away long enough to catch enough little auks to make a new undershirt. Then I would give the shirt to Bozi." But she knew she would never have the courage to give it to him—it was only an idea which was born in her head.

When the food was cooked it was poured into two large bowls which Bozi and Elias carried into the middle room, where there was a table. There were many plates there, and forks and spoons lay by their sides. Bozi put the meat on the plates and then called his guests. It was apparent that the meat was already cut into small pieces, so it was unnecessary to use the knives. It was just as though it had been chewed in advance. Several of them whispered to each other that, while it might be good to eat, it certainly would not make them fat!

Several times Bozi went to Ivalu and offered her food, but she immediately pushed others, who were older than she, ahead of her. She did not want it said that she ate before her elders. Bozi even offered her food before the men had been served and they all laughed very much about that.

When Merquzaq had finished he handed his plate to Ivalu, but she did not want to walk through the room and show that as yet she had had nothing.

Luckily Elias had kept his eye on her, and now he took her plate and heaped food on it. She went into a corner and began to eat. She wanted to be alone for a little while, because it brought back the remembrance of being on Peary's ship as a child.

She found out that the food which had been given her did not taste good at all. It was salty and bitter, but her companions told her it was because the palates of white men were thicker-skinned than those of other people. If there were no bitter things in their food, then the taste could not penetrate to their heads. But then Bozi came with more little pots and around these was thick paper with pretty colors on it. In them were big, yellow berries of a size they had never seen before, and they swam in a thick, good-tasting soup. And when Ivalu took one of these in her mouth, it seemed to her that the white men must be gentle and without the capacity of anger, if they could produce such good food.

When everything was eaten, Bozi brought out a mighty tea kettle. In many more cups than one could count he poured warm tea, and on the table stood sugar in two big glass boxes from which everyone could take as much as he wanted. Unfortunately, Bozi did not even think of putting sugar into the tea of his guests himself! They could not understand this, as he had been willing to go to great pains about everything else. They were uncomfortable, and did

not want to be bad mannered, so they put only a very
little of the sweet into the drink. A little boy named
Napsar, who was the son of Torngé's wife, (but
whose father was thought to be a white man, as the
boy's hair was not black, but reddish!), had no such
feeling of shame. He stood for a long time in front of
the sugar boxes, pouring spoonful after spoonful into
his tea while Bozi watched. Napsar thought he was
showing the white man how greatly he valued his
hospitality, so he kept on putting more sugar into
his tea. Bozi laughed at him, took the sugar box, and
went around, holding out the sugar to each one in
turn. When he came to Ivalu, she felt so strange she
did not even want to look at the sugar. Her face became hot and she acted as though she were angry,
and told him she did not want any. When he still
held the sugar box in front of her and said he did not
understand her, she took a very little sugar on the tip
of her spoon and put it into her tea. She wished he
wouldn't look at her for she felt a longing in her body
for a lot of sugar. This made her ashamed of herself,
and she turned to her friends and talked insultingly
without knowing for whom the insults were intended.

Bozi gave them some hard bread to eat with their
tea, and as they ate it they decided that the women
who had baked it must have a great deal of sugar,
as they had mixed a lot of it in the dough.

While they were eating they did not talk, but they

noticed that Bozi did not consider it unfriendly to talk and drink tea at the same time. He began to ask about many things and his friendliness spread to the others. His remarkable interest in names persisted, for he went around and told them all their names. Sometimes he made a mistake, and when he came to Ivalu he called her Avordungiak. It made her angry, because the others laughed and looked at her, and she wished she were far away.

Now Bozi had a new idea. He told Ivalu and two other young women to come to another part of the house with him. They followed him uncertainly, as they did not know what he wanted, and all the rest of the women came along to see. Bozi took with him all the things they had used for eating, pointed to the plates and cups and spoons, and then at a few large pots which were wide and flat. The young women became flaming red and almost cried with shame, because they thought he wanted to give all these things to them—a proposition for the three of them while the others were all watching. It was so indecent that Ivalu decided to move to another settlement as soon as she could.

They looked down on the ground, and when he took hold of their shoulders and pushed them gently, they became angry, for they were young women who must defend themselves against a man. Immediately, however, Elias explained what Bozi wanted. All these cups, plates, and spoons were to be washed in the big pots. This was to happen every time after they ate, and this time it was these three young women who should do this unusual cleaning. The men began to laugh and said that this same procedure was the custom aboard ship, and the married women came closer to see what was going to happen.

Bozi soon realized that it would be impossible to get the young women to do this, for Elias explained to him that they did not wish to break the customs of the people when everybody was watching. So he gave up the plan and took them into the largest room of the house. Here he explained to them that all the goods in the cases did not belong to him himself, but to certain persons in his land, who were greater than he. They had sent these things to get fox skins for them. Still, he wanted to give each one of them a pipe and two pieces of tobacco. If, in the future, more tobacco or other things were wanted, they were to be paid for. After they had thought about this for a little, Uvdluriak said he completely accepted Bozi's idea. "I will tell my people that all of your goods are to be had for payment," he said.

Now they were all given fire for their pipes and the smoke in the room became so thick it collected under the roof like a cloud. It reminded them of a ship they had seen come sailing over the sea, and which made smoke that drove it through the water.

Bozi had a big box on which he laid round, black plates with holes in the middle. When they were set in motion, a remarkable noise was produced and Elias said it was the joy of the white men. All of the guests listened for a long time and were delighted by it, but suddenly Bozi stepped to Ivalu, held her around the body, and pulled her around the room with him. She resisted strongly, but he began to run around with her and turned her again and again until her legs weakened and she was ready to sink to the ground. But, by now, she was so angry at his impudence that she ran out the door. In the hall she laughed aloud from anger and ran home to Uvdluriak's house, where she lay down on the plank bed and nearly cried.

Bozi stopped and looked after her, but, as he turned, he saw that nobody was laughing any more. They had not understood what he was trying to do. Now Elias told them that the dances of the white men were danced when the box made a noise, and that both a man and a woman were necessary. Now Merquzaq asked whether that was practiced in full light and when many people looked on. Elias say "yes", and they were all very much ashamed for white men.

Shortly, they got the idea that Bozi's hospitality was at an end. Their visit had already lasted longer than it was customary for them to stay in the houses of their friends.

"The event of going home has come," said Uvd-luriak, and went, as usual, ahead. They all followed him, and outside of the house they stopped for a while and looked at the weather. They decided that, for the next few days, they would try to catch some walrus on the far side of the fjord.

Chapter Ten

THERE is a big difference, in going out to catch walruses, whether one goes in a large wooden boat with many people rowing, or goes all alone in a *kayak*, in which there is only a thin skin separating one from the animal. They went in Bozi's boat, laughing and talking. Three *kayaks* were being paddled alongside, but when the wind came up and Bozi set the sails, these *kayaks* were tied behind and towed like slain animals.

When they reached the island they went ashore and climbed to the highest point to look around. They could hear the animals snorting on the other side of the island. There were many walruses over there, playing in the water. They would dive, flipping their tails at their fellows, and disappear in the deep. When they came up again they would take two long whistling breaths, and lie there for a while, enjoying the air, before they would again dive to the bottom to fill their stomachs.

Uvdluriak was the first to kill a walrus since Bozi arrived. It was a wonderful sight for the white men to see him paddle toward his intended prey, bent forward in his *kayak* so that he could hardly be seen. Every time the animal turned its back on him and swam a little further out of range, he raised his spear. The animal had not noticed him; it raised its tail, undisturbed, and dived to the bottom. Uvdluriak rmeained lying still, waiting for it to fill itself with mussels and then come up again. When it did he was closer to it, and set out rapidly after his victim. This one was enormous, so old that its skin was almost white and so fat that its back was high out of the water.

Uvdluriak paddled up close to it. The animal was thinking of nothing. It felt secure in its strength, knowing that no one could resist it in battle because of its thick skin and powerful tusks. Then it felt its back pierced by Uvdluriak's harpoon, and, furious with pain and at having been disturbed, reared straight up in the water. But Uvdluriak had thrown his harpoon well. The catch bladder, which was tied to the line, was pulled down into the water and slowed up the animal. Now Uvdluriak was concerned only with getting away before the enraged beast sank its tusks into the *kayak* and pulled him down to the death which hides on the bottom of the sea.

"Ak! Look, he has harpooned," shouted those in the boat. "Uvdluriak has caught one!" They rowed toward him as fast as they could, to help him kill the animal.

In front of the bow of the heavy boat there was a lot of foam, and the three *kayaks* waited tensely for the walrus to again come to the surface. After they waited a short time, they heard it snort and groan near by. The wounded animal needed more air. The catch bladder made it difficult for him to stay down, and moved the harpoon in the wound, and the pain tired out the walrus. There was no more air in its body and it had to rest on the surface a while before it would fill itself with enough more to dive and get away.

Torngé, who sat in the second *kayak,* took advantage of this to paddle up close. He drove his harpoon in near the other wound. Again there was a furious whipping of the water, but now there were two catch bladders pulling against the animal and he was doomed, even if he should manage to tear one of them to pieces with his teeth. Uvdluriak thrust his spear between the walrus' ribs and slipped neatly away. The larger boat came close, and Bozi took his gun and shot the walrus dead through the eye.

"Ak! Joy, joy! We have caught a walrus!" they all shouted. They all started to talk about it at once, nobody listening to anybody else. But they all had high praise for Bozi, who shot a walrus through the brain with the first shot he had fired in this new land.

"Ak! That is always the luck of beginners," Merquzaq said. He sat in the boat and gave the catchers in the *kayaks* good advice with regard to making the animal fast. He had killed walruses before either of them had been born. It was difficult to row with a walrus dragging behind, but in a little while it became more difficult, because they had two to tow.

Samik caught the other one. A walrus came up in the vicinity of the boat and Samik spotted it and paddled swiftly toward it. It was an enormous bull, one of the old ones which always come up with their eyes closed, because they are too proud to look around and be prepared for danger. It swam slowly ahead, puffing and snorting, and Samik rowed at it head on, which is the most dangerous way. But he held the harpoon firmly in his right hand, hurled it over the *kayak*-stem, and it went over the head of the animal and lodged in its back, quivering there for an instant until the shaft broke off above the point.

The white man could see, aye, Bozi and all the others, too, could see that Samik belonged to those who had no fear in their bodies, and that he attacked a walrus head on and harpooned it without waiting for it to turn its head away or have its back to the catcher.

Now the wind started to blow a little, and they sat in the boat and talked about the many times one had to flee toward the shore when the wind whipped up the waves. The old folks used to say it was the revenge of the walruses for killing two of their number. But now, as they sat in the boat, Ajorzalik, the medicine man, said that they could save the powerful formula which stilled the wind and smoothed the waves for another time. For now they were in a sturdy boat, and could laugh with scorn when the foam appeared on the waves.

When they reached shore the tide was coming in, so they decided to postpone skinning the animals and carried them as far up the beach as was possible. They cut some meat from the walruses and made ready to cook a pot full and be merry. As soon as the tide made it possible they went down to the animals, stuck their knives into them, and cut out enormous portions. The skinning was an interesting sight to Bozi.

"This is your meat," Merquzaq said to him, as soon as the first one was cut up. Bozi thanked them and asked them if they wanted payment for the meat he received. They all laughed and told him that no payment was wanted, and turned to skin and carve the second animal. Its stomach was full of wonderful mussels, and these they took out and ate. They taught Bozi how to hold them in his hand and rinse them with sea water, so that they would be clean and inviting to him. This second walrus also gave a large quantity of meat to Bozi. "I thank you," he said, "and I am glad that my dogs will have food when winter comes."

They killed another walrus, and again Bozi showed he was grateful for receiving meat. He seemed very surprised. They laughed at him again, and one of

the young men said that each time he received a
share of the catch he could give them some tobacco.
Merquzaq felt sorry for the white men, who came
with other customs from those of the people, and he
told Bozi that he must not be grateful for receiving
meat.

"You are a man with dogs that need food, and it
is necessary that you receive a share of the catch.
Here, in this country, we don't want payment for
what is a man's right. It is not a gift that you receive,
but your share, and, when you catch a walrus, all the
meat that is not yours is ours. It is best that everyone has a right to share in the catch, for through
presents humility is created, and through the whip,
dogs. Often one who has nothing feels himself
whipped if he has to be grateful for things which he
needs."

When they rowed home the women were standing up waiting for them. Women are always full of
talk and cannot be satisfied with what their eyes show
them, so one of them called out that, surely, the boats
came home with catch. At this Ivalu said she wished
Bozi had also caught, for it must be wonderful to
taste meat from the catch of a white man. Several
of them turned and looked at her, and she was embarrassed and decided to say nothing else.

Now the call came from the boat that it was Uvdluriak and Samik who had caught. The wives of the

two men immediately went down to the boat and started chattering that the dogs should be kept away, and that it was a nuisance to get meat into the house at this time of year; they said they wished they were married to men who did not burden their wives with the cooking of meat and other work.

Bozi went into his house and from his closet took one of the paper bunches which were held together at one end. He sat down to his table and began to turn his thoughts into lines which he put down on the paper while he still remembered them. Many thoughts lived in the head of the white man, for he sat there a long time without speaking.

Now they cooked over a huge fire. This was one of the meals of big catches, when they all ate together and at which the men pass meat to their wives and children. Bozi saw Merquzaq take a piece of meat and pass it to an old woman, who stood near Ivalu. Ivalu was young and her turn would not come until the next cooking, after most had had their fill. But Bozi took a piece, handed the inviting bite to Ivalu, and said, "Please—this should be eaten by you." Everybody laughed at this and Ivalu pulled her hand back.

Many days passed now, during which she did not visit his house, and, when others went there to look at the interesting things, Ivalu stayed behind, saying she wanted to straighten out the tent or sew new clothes for her little sisters.

Every evening, when the others returned home, they told her something new about his house. Each time they went they got tea or coffee and often bread with it. He had peculiar, bending bread, which was twisted into knots as though it were made from stiffened gut. These twists were full of little black things; one could see that the white men's lice were being baked into their food. The children laughed and were amused at eating lice from the land of the white men. They thought their hair would become lighter, as the lice must contain the blood of the men on whom they had lived.

As autumn came, the young women went up to the lake to catch salmon-trout. Ivalu cut a hole in the ice and had a little bait-fish her grandfather had carved for her from a walrus tooth. Each woman stood by her hole, and, so as not to scare away any game, they did not speak, but contented themselves with the amusement of making signs to one another with their arms and knees, and only smiled at each other.

Then they saw Bozi and Elias coming. They had been out hunting snow chickens and were returning with many birds. Bozi came across the lake to Ivalu, who had a fish longer than her arm lying by her on the ice. It was the biggest salmon-trout caught in the settlement since Bozi's arrival, and he asked her if he could have it, as he was tired of eating meat.

Ivalu was ashamed that a man had come to ask her for food, and she meant not to tell anyone about it. But Elias heard it, and he would tell about it, and then people would come and ask her: How was it with the white man, who came to you for food? Didn't he want anything else but that? She took her salmon and gave them to Bozi, and said she did not know if they were edible, that she herself had never tasted them—she was only standing there and catching them.

He laughed and, taking his hand out of his mitten, stroked her face three times, and she could feel the warmth of his fingers. Then he pulled a few snow chickens from his bundle and gave them to her. He left, but before he had gone very far he turned and called back to her. He asked why she didn't visit him more often, and said he hoped she would come to his house soon, so that they could eat together.

As soon as he disappeared behind the slope, the other women came running to her, laughing and talking in a peculiar way. That night there was talk in all the houses that Ivalu had bargained about food with the white man, and had been so intimidated that she had exchanged fish for birds. As if it were allowed to exchange meat from the water for meat from the land! When Merquzaq heard about it he went to her and spoke angrily, and took the snow chickens away from her. He said that the lake would feel anger at this kind of an exchange and the land animals would flee, angrily leaving only fish for the people. Therefore it is wrong to exchange one for the other, or to cook them in the same pot.

Ivalu said nothing. She realized that he would be angry if she told him that the wishes of a white man were so strong that a poor woman could not resist them. Merquzaq would not understand if she told him that Bozi had not given her a snow chicken as payment—but only to thank her.

Chapter Eleven

ONE day, while the ice was still too new for one to expect visiting sleds, two black specks were discovered on the other side of the fjords, moving very slowly. They were Mayark and Minik, coming from the north where they had spent the summer in visiting and feasting as honored guests, and eating the catch of strangers. Now they were returning. Mayark's family were at Cape York, but they had heard that there was a white man living in the settlement, so they stopped and went straight to his house.

"Herewith one has come to visit," Mayark said, and sat down on a bench. But Minik stepped forward, and it was apparent he was of equal birth with the white man. He spoke wonderful words in a strange language, and held out his hand exactly like Bozi. They clasped each other's hands and held tightly. Then they sat down to talk. Whenever one of them said anything, he smiled at his own words, although it is unbecoming for one to laugh at the words one speaks.

Later Minik explained that he was received with great cordiality. "We place great value on hearing one another's experiences," he said, "so I will stay here in the settlement and let Mayark journey on alone."

Shortly one could see that Minik was thinking of women.

It was Ivalu who gave him the occasion to show this, and it happened in this manner: one day Samik grabbed Ivalu around the waist, lifted her on his shoulder, and started to carry her to his house, which happened to be empty.

Ivalu was paralyzed by fury and fear. Everybody was afraid of the big Samik. As a child, there had been robbery in his life, and several times there had been murder. So she did not dare to bite him. She screamed and struggled and cried that she did not want to belong to him. When Samik tried to push her in through the house entrance, she resisted with all her might. Samik got angry at her resistance, took hold of her head and forced it forward so that it hurt her neck. But she spread her legs and braced her feet against the edge of the door.

When a woman is really unwilling to give in to a man she becomes very strong. She resisted him and screamed. Minik heard her and came running, forgetting that he was only a young man against the big Samik. Perhaps he had forgotten, after having been away from his land for so long, that in a quarrel the young must always give in to the older. He grabbed Samik by the shoulders from behind, pulling him backwards so that he fell into the snow. He was shouting angrily as he did this.

Ivalu got up and remained standing at a little distance, watching the men fight. Minik was young and strong and his life among the white men had taught him how to fight. Aiming at Samik's face, he hit him on the chin with such force that the big man fell back and remained lying on the ground.

"It seems that he is dead," Ivalu said, and was frightened that she had been the cause of big animosity among men.

That night Minik went to Bozi's house and had a long conversation with him. Later there was talk in all the houses that Minik had moved in as a helper to the white man.

It was not quite certain that it was an advantage to have Minik as a house partner, for the people could often hear Bozi speaking loudly to him in a strange language. It was not the language of Bozi's own country. Evidently there were many sorts of people in the land of the white men, and they lived far from one another.

And one day when Minik was angry at Bozi, he told the settlement that Bozi was not a great master. He said Bozi's country was far smaller than Peary's and without the same power. Peary was always a master. He said "Please take this," when he wanted to give something away. Bozi, however, gave things only to those who gave things in exchange, and the skins which he received from the people were of far greater value than the tobacco and sugar which he gave in payment.

One evening Ivalu was missing. Her plank bed was empty until very late, and when she came home it was in a great hurry, as though she were fleeing from somebody.

At sunset she had taken a few snares and gone to the hill to set them across two little ditches through which hares ran. When she went back, later, a hare had been caught. She took it down, and on her way home walked around the point, so that she could not be seen from Bozi's house. She intended to cut across a frozen little inlet—but Minik came over the ice, riding in a great hurry.

His dogs noticed Ivalu before he did. He tried to turn them aside, but his ability was less than the desire of the dogs, so they kept on heading toward her. Suddenly she found herself faced by many dogs who had stopped, embarrassed when they found she was only a human being and not food.

Minik jumped from his sled and grabbed hold of her.

"Let me go!" she cried. "Can't you see I'm on my way home and that I'm carrying a hare?"

Minik did not answer. He only laughed his shrill laugh, picked her up and started to carry her to the sled. She got angry and fought him, but he laid her on the sled and sat down on her so that with his thighs he could hold her body tightly. "Hock! Hock!" he shouted at his dogs, and they leaped forward.

Minik turned to her and tried to press his face against hers.

"Let go!" she cried. "Drive home to your house, you who come back without catch! Why do you want to make yourself laughed at by coming home with a woman?"

"I don't make myself ridiculous," Minik said. "I am just sorry for you who walk alone here and are without a man. So now you shall be my wife."

Ivalu fought with silent anger and struggled on the sled.

"Don't you see I've lost my hare?" she cried. But Minik did not care.

She began to mock him.

"You come back without seals, so of course you must take a poor, defenseless woman, so as to return home with something! It must be very amusing to be strong enough to overcome one who is weaker."

Minik got angry and hit her on the arm with his bare fist.

"Ak! go on and hit me," she cried. "Why not use your whip? It is indeed the lot of the woman who is to become your wife to be fattened with beatings instead of food! If you hit me in the face it will swell up, and it will look as though you had fed me well.

Then other women will be envious of me. Ak! What a joy! What a man I got, indeed!''

They reached the rocks which led to the houses. Those who stood outside saw a team of galloping dogs fly past, pulling a sled on which lay a man and woman wrestling. Suddenly the sled hit a bump on the beach and they were flung off, rolling in opposite directions.

"Ak you miserable dogs!" Minik roared, and jumped to his feet. But Ivalu slipped away. She moved so fast that her feet did not know how they got over the jagged beach-ice and climbed up the slope. She slipped into the house tunnel like a fox into his hole. When she came in, her grandparents did not ask her any questions. She was a young woman who had been out to her snares and, as she came home without a hare, they did not wish to embarrass her by asking the result of her catch.

The men went out on the smooth ice to catch. Uvdluriak had taken Bozi along and was teaching him. Under their feet they had tied bearskin soles so that they could walk noiselessly. Glazed-ice catch is very profitable, when there are many seals. One goes out on the ice and remains standing still. When the breathing of the seals is heard in a nearby breathing hole, one moves toward it slowly. When the animal starts to blow, one lifts a foot. The seal says *"Fuh!"*

in the hole, and as he makes the sound one puts his foot down. Another *"Fuh!"* and one takes another step, and so one moves closer. But as soon as one hears the seal dive, one must not move a single limb. The whole skin of the seal is like a big ear under water, and he hears everything that happens on the ice.

Uvdluriak had explained all this to Bozi, and now Bozi was standing right over a breathing hole. There was a *"Fuh!"* and the seal blew water over the thin ice. And one more. He lifted his harpoon as high as he could stretch his arm, and, when the seal breathed again, he drove the weapon down into the water. He put so much strength into the blow that he fell forward on the ice, and he had hit his mark.

The catchers were so far away from home that they could find no reason for returning that night. They decided to stay on a small island, and Bozi learned how to make camp. The cold was severe, and in his own country he would have thought it impossible to remain there without shelter or heat.

An enormous blubber fire was lighted and over it meat was cooked in two little pots. When it was done, a man took out the hot pieces of meat and laid them on the ice to cool. After they had all eaten they drank the soup and the pot was also handed to Bozi. His face and hands got black with soot and they all laughed and told him that now he looked just like one of them.

"He who is black with soot brings home catch," Uvdluriak said.

They retired and slept on their sleds. Bozi heard them snore on both sides of him, but soon it began to freeze and he got up and walked up and down to keep warm. He met Minik, who had gone to look after his dogs. So they stopped and began to speak to each other. For Minik had lived in the land of the white men, and white men are always full of talk.

There was no great friendship between the two men. Some said that Bozi did not wish Minik to be a white man like himself. Others thought that Minik was without happiness because he had met someone who was better than he, and that his mocking words about Bozi's riches had envy as their cause. But then why had Minik not brought many possessions with him when he had returned?

"I have thought of getting married," Minik said. "Will you allow me to bring Ivalu into the house?"

"Who?" Bozi asked. "Kazaluk's daughter?"

"Yes," Minik said. "I intend to marry her, and I have talked about it to her family. If you will permit it, I want to bring her into your house. Then she can sew and cook for both of us and for Elias, and be the woman of the house."

That was what he said, and Bozi thought it had all been settled. It would be pleasant to have a woman to take care of their things, and sew and cook. He gave Minik permission and said, "I like Ivalu. She, of all the women here, most resembles the women of my own country. Her expression is so intelligent that she even seems to understand our talk."

Bozi said that home, in his country, there was a woman waiting to become his. He only had to make enough money here so that he could return and get married.

"When will you bring Ivalu into our house?" he asked.

"I do not know. I will have to catch a few foxes for a coat for her, first. It is not becoming that I should give her her first clothes made from a stranger's catch—even if I don't care whether the natives laugh at me."

Minik always talked like that. There was always a hidden begging in any of his propositions, and he always called his fellow catchers "natives." He wanted to be considered a white man. That was why he had moved into Bozi's house. He had wanted to from the beginning, but never wanted to ask it directly.

"It will be best if the two of you live in the little room," Bozi said. "Then Elias can move into my room."

The next morning when they woke up, Bozi and Minik were freezing. The others laughed at them, and Merquzaq said it was because of the weak food they ate in Bozi's house. "Cook meat and eat it," he said. "When you have derived heat and strength from it, the cold will no longer have any power over you."

Clouds moved up on the sky, looking like black mountains. The northern lights jumped up and down in long rows, without the strength to give daylight. They are the stillborn children, who run up and down the sky, playing with their navel strings. They run from one end of the sky to the other, in long rows, and sometimes they kick a star which falls down and breaks. At times their laughter can be felt in the air—but without anyone hearing it.

"The stillborn children do everything upside down," Merquzaq said. "Their laughter cannot be heard, it is seen. And their light gives no warmth. They were born not to live, and they never died because they never breathed."

It started to blow. When the wind whistles in one's ear, one cannot hear the breathing of the seals. So they loaded their sleds, harnessed the dogs, and drove home.

Elias took care of Bozi's house, and when they returned there was heat and food. Bozi had decided that all the members of the settlement should have a feast. Now they knew him better than the first time they had been invited. They went back and forth, from one room to another. The old women preferred

to sit in the room where the food was being cooked,
and they whispered to each other that, when visiting sleds came in the winter, delicate food would be
prepared here. They told Bozi that their palates were
happy over the expectation of tasting his food.

Suddenly they heard loud talk from the room
which one reached through the passage. It was a
woman's voice—Ivalu's. She cried out, and came
running out of the room so fast that they understood
what had happened. Minik had said that he and
Ivalu were to move in there, and he thought of marry-
ing her.

Ivalu ran home. On the way her anger grew and
turned not only against Minik but against the whole
house of Bozi. She thought of how different things
were than they were on Peary's ship. Bozi's ship did
not contain treasures, like Peary's, so it was only
natural that the men were also of a less pleasant nature. She began to cry, because she was without a
man. Only now did she think back to the time when
she was married. When she and Mitzerk had no
longer known embarrassment in each other's presence, they had, in the evenings, often spoken about
the things that happened during the day. One knew
how the other felt. True, he told her that everything
she said was only a woman's opinion, but still she
longed for him and now she knew what lonesomeness
was. She had found out that those who are alone

always feel a hunger in their bodies and therefore are easily angered.

But ak! here on the settlement was no young man to whom she wished to belong. Minik thought he was a white man because he could tell of things in far away countries. But his talk was carried by staggering words, and for a man who has forgotten the language of his own country one can hardly have respect. So she decided she did not want to marry Minik. And a woman should be able to say who her husband would be, whose skins she wanted to prepare, and with whom she wished to grow old in case many years should be given her.

As she thought of these things her anger cooled, but although she knew they were eating good food at Bozi's, she did not want to go back. None of the others could appreciate the white men's food as well as she. It was really because she thought so often of his sweet food that she didn't go there more often. Now she must remain without a guest meal, and be disappointed.

Suddenly she heard shouts from the ice. A sled came speeding up, and then another. She could tell from their voices that the men were Apilak and Tatiak, her former brothers-in-law, arriving for a visit. Ak! she didn't care to meet them. She didn't like them, because they had robbed her of her possessions, which had belonged to her husband. Even the things which he had given her himself, they had taken away.

When they came up to the settlement Ivalu stepped to the house entrance. But they had brought no women along, so she had to go into the house and wait.

Apilak came in and saw that she was alone. "Herewith one comes to visit," he said. "Ak! a woman is ready to receive us. What joy for a man who has been so long away from his wife!"

"Be quiet!" Ivalu said. "Go and see the people of the settlement. They are at the white man's house— and he forbids the attacking of women!"

She felt a resentment against the family of her husband. Mitzerk was altogether different from them, and he often talked to her about moving away from the others, who were so possessive. Once Apilak had asked Mitzerk to exchange wives with him, as he wanted to sleep with Ivalu.

"That helps the catch," he said to Mitzerk. But Mitzerk refused, and so she remained a stranger to her brother-in-law, to this one's continuous anger.

Tatiak also came in with his helper, Uzugodark, a deaf and mute boy.

"Bo, bo, bo," was all he could say, as he had never been able to speak words. He was badly dressed. His trousers had no hair in front or back, and his reindeer coat was worn bare. One could see he was happy to come into a house.

Ivalu was glad when they left. They left Uzugo-dark with her, although he would have liked to go along.

Over Bozi's house hovered merriment and the odor of coffee, as usual. The smoke lay thick up under the roof, and people were laughing, when the door opened. Apilak and Tatiak came in—two men who could tell them all about the happenings on the lee side of the land.

Chapter Twelve

Apilak told them about Uvizakazek, a man who had been killed up north during the past summer Apilak and a man named Zigdlu had killed him in order to keep their women in peace. Now Apilak was seeking protection from Bozi, for Uvizakazek had a brother, called the Fat-Cheeked, who wanted revenge on Apilak and Zigdlu. Apilak felt that he was safe, now, but he was very sorry for Zigdlu, who was in great danger.

After he had finished talking, Bozi told him that they had committed a very bad deed in killing Uvizakazek. But a new murder must not follow this one, he said, and he was going north to talk to the Fat-Cheeked. He wanted peace among the people, and wanted to help them when they could not settle their own difficulties.

The following morning he began to make preparations for his trip, and Kazaluk came to put his things in order. Old Ama had sewn him a fur sack in which he could put his things on the sled, and so keep the snow off them.

"I just remembered," Bozi told Minik, "that I have a barrel of that crazy-making drink. It is better if we put it into bottles."

Minik was eager to do this. He often asked Bozi for a cup of this drink, which Bozi called "whiskey."

Bozi himself had no desire to drink it and warned Minik that it was to be used only in case of illness or sometimes to create happiness which would not come by itself. Minik said he was right, but that he himself had been used to handling this kind of drink in the great countries.

Bozi got busy writing into his book. After a while they heard Minik singing in a foreign language, and just then visitors arrived. It was big Torngé and Uvdluriak. When they went into Minik's room they found him lying on the floor. His eyes looked like a clouded sky, there was drivel around his mouth, and he lay there and sang, not noticing that the door had opened and people had come in.

Bozi ran to him and shook him, and now one could see there were many bottles on the floor. Minik even had a bottle in his hand. It was clear that he had been drinking and had not thought that the strength in the drink was greater than his own.

"Minik!" Bozi said angrily, "you drank the whiskey!" And in the language of the white men he said many things, and his face showed he was very angry.

"Leave him lying there," he said to the others. "These bottles should have been put away. I will take care, from now on, that their power does not hit people with illness!"

He took the bottles and put them in the closet

where he kept all his tasty things. "Let Minik sleep," he said again.

Minik could sing no longer, and now his strength left him. Then he vomited and got very sick. They offered him water, but he said, "I do not want to drink that which flows in rivers! I want to drink from the bottles! My sickness demands it."

The air where Minik lay was peculiar and made them dizzy. But Bozi said that air did not kill a person, so they let Minik sleep and went inside to talk about the journey.

Uvdluriak was to go with Bozi, but that evening he told the white man that the southwest wind wanted to come up. It was still calm on the plain where they lived, but further inland clouds were settling over the mountains. These mountains always covered themselves with a cloud coat to protect themselves from bad weather. They were a part of nature, and knew everything which was going to happen ahead of time, so the people should pay attention to their warnings.

Uzugodark, the deaf mute, had also come visiting. He was full of lice and he had no one to look after him. His married sister lived in the north, but she was not good to him because he ate so much and provided nothing. So now he was on his way to the windward side where there was a relative who would take him in. He was a boy who should have been killed when it was seen that he would be incapable of supporting himself, but his mother was a bad woman who did not think of her child, and had let him live. She had grown to love him so much that she could not kill him herself, and would not allow anyone else to put a noose around his neck and hang him. Now he had grown, and although at times he was useful, mostly he was a burden. The people amused themselves by teasing him. When he was in their houses they would present him with their most valuable belongings, but he couldn't understand what they said, and did not take the presents, which amused them a great deal.

Now he sat in a corner and let his eyes wander around the big house. Every time Bozi smiled at him he laughed and made a sound, although it was not the custom of the people to exclaim aloud when someone smiled. He had his mittens on, of which Uvdluriak said he was very proud, but they were miserable and full of holes. But Ivalu was sewing a new pair for him, and she had fixed his stockings, so that now he laughed, stroked her hair, and made sounds which were meant to be happy words.

"But why does no one give him things?" Bozi asked. "You have so many skins—have you nothing for him?"

"Ak! yes, why isn't he given things? We all have skins. But people are like that— they give no skins where they get nothing for them. It is the lot of orphans that they must wait until they can earn enough for themselves."

They all said people were very strange, and then they stopped talking and remained quiet. They were thinking that Bozi's words sounded like a reproach.

Bozi took the boy into the sleeping room, and one could hear him saying, "Mo! Mo!" And when he came out he appeared like a white man, and was to be envied. It made everybody laugh. For Uzugodark was wearing white men's clothes. His jacket was nice and freshly washed, and underneath he had two more. His pants were thin and smooth, with no hair on them at all, and he had small, low shoes like the ones they wore on the ships. Bozi said he wanted to keep the deaf mute in his house as a helper. At this the men said they understood that a white man was always willing to help, and they had already thought that Bozi would surely help a boy who had no relatives.

The white man turned to Torngé's wife and said, "Here are skins for trousers and boots, and rabbit skins for stockings."

He wanted her to sew new clothes for Uzugodark. But at this she got angry.

"It is better that a more capable one than I should sew for such a distinguished man, for such a big hand must surely be accustomed to bring home many skins! His clothes should be much finer than those which I could deliver! As long as Ama and Kazaluk are to do the sewing for you, it is better that they should also sew for the fine man that Uzugodark has become!"

At this they all laughed and said that the angry woman was right, but Ama said that Ivalu would sew, and would come next day to try on the clothes.

The next morning, when Bozi got up, Minik was still lying in bed. He said he was sick in the head, and must have a half cup of whiskey. But Bozi said "No!", and closed his ears. Then Minik started to beg, and finally Bozi poured a drink into his cup and gave it to him. After Minik had drunk it, he said it had been too little. He pointed to his neck and showed how short a distance it had gone down. If it had been only a little more, then it would have reached his stomach and cured him completely. Bozi again poured a little into the cup, and, after Minik had drunk that, he went out without eating.

The snowstorm raged, just as Uvdluriak had said it would. During the day it got no better for journey-ing, but visitors fought their way through the storm and came into Bozi's house. They saw that Uzugo-dark had been given a place at the table, with a plate and a cup which were filled whenever they were empty. Then Apilak decided it had been wrong of him to bring the deaf mute here. But the boy was very happy, and kept laughing and making his strange sounds of joy.

Ivalu came in. Her fur coat was covered with snow, but she dusted it off in the house corridor. She pulled back her cowl and was very pretty, with her cheeks all red and her hair blowing around her head.

She had been sitting home, that morning, sewing on Uzugodark's things, thinking that the boy belonged among those for whom one feels sorry, and pleased that Bozi had sent word that she should sew new clothes for him. Then Minik had come in, his eyes looking as though sleep had become master over them, his mouth like the jaws of a walrus, and a peculiar bad smell coming from his throat. He stepped straight to her as though he did not know that there was anyone else in her house, grabbed her by the breast and started to say insulting things. She had kicked him off and crawled back behind the bed plank, but Minik had followed her, groping for her naked legs. She slipped to one side, to keep on the floor and out of his way, and his eyes became even more cloudy and he could not catch her, for he was really full of sleep as his eyes had shown.

Ivalu had sewn all the evening before and from early that morning, and the things were almost ready.

"One must go to the big house," she said, "Words about the sewing must be spoken to the white man."

At this Minik began to say that Bozi's power was

very small compared to that which Minik had seen in other white men. So, he said, he had decided to tell the white whale catchers to send him large quantities of goods so he could trade with the people. Then, next year, the whale catchers could receive all the foxes which now Bozi intended to buy.

Ivalu was a grown up woman and her thoughts were like a man's. Ak! so these were his intentions—this was why he had returned! He also said he had come without these things to trade so that he could see how much fox trapping there was before he began with his big trading. But, Ivalu thought, that must be against Bozi's wish. He would not want another to do what he was doing himself.

"One goes to the big house," she said again. "There decisions are made—and what Minik has said will be told to Bozi."

The storm was blowing hard against her. She had to bend forward, and sometimes turn her back against the wind in order to breathe. She was not going visiting without having business to attend to. She was a woman going to deliver things for which she might, perhaps, receive payment. Yes, surely he would give her tea and bread. And he always gave her a cup which he had first dried with his own hands on a white thing which hung over the warmer-upper.

Now she stood in front of the house. It seemed to her proper that she was there, even though she came without having sewed on the waistband of the trousers. After all, no one could tell how wide pants were to be. She wanted to finish them here at Bozi's house, and deliver them to him before she left. Yes, she would sit there and sew, and maybe she would suddenly say, "Ak! its' too bad that I have forgotten my curved knife. May I borrow something for cutting?" And then Bozi would give her his own knife. It would be wonderful to hold his knife in her hand!

Bozi went to meet her and took her hand, which now was understood to be his habit of greeting. But she heard the women whispering and noticed that all eyes were looking at her. Therefore it was not easy for her to speak her thoughts, but she did explain that she must know how thick Uzugodark was around the belly. Then she could finish the sewing of his trousers right away.

Bozi began to laugh and said that Uzugodark had gotten a bigger belly, and at this all the others laughed, too. Ivalu forgot her embarrassment completely, because what the white man said was so amusing.

Now Bozi put his hand on her shoulder and led her into the inner room and called Uzugodark. The boy did not understand anything, he only laughed while Ivalu was pointing at him and at the trousers. She showed with her hand that he should take off the trousers he wore and put these on.

Bozi stood by and laughed. He had given her the fine bearskins which he had determined to have for his own pants. Then she measured the belly of the boy to see how thick he was. While doing this, her hand touched Bozi's. She felt that his hand was warm, and it was as though she had put her hand on her own body, so familiar did the touch seem to her. They looked at each other and laughed into each other's eyes. But then Uzugodark began to howl with happiness, and the other women stole in. All joy left Ivalu and her face lost its smile.

"One wishes a belt," she said. "A belt has been forgotten, and left at home." And Elias brought her a thin seal belt to pull through the linen.

It was not at all amusing to sit there and sew. She had forgotten that others were to be there. But presently she remembered what she had meant to say.

"One needs a knife—something has to be cut," she said, and it went just as she had planned. Bozi put his hand in his pocket and pulled out a knife, one of those that can be snapped together. It was warm and smooth to feel, and, while she was cutting, she felt the warmth of the white man pass into her hand. She held the knife a long time, as if the cutting were giving her trouble.

"At last the trousers are finished," she said finally. "It has taken much too long, but you turned to an incapable one when you wanted to have them sewn."

She wanted to show the other women that she was an ordered helper, and had not asked to do this work for him. She wanted her words to arouse objection in him, so that he would say things which could be cherished and retold in other settlements. "Ivalu," they would say, "the one who sewed things for the house partner of the white man, and who finished more quickly than it was possible for anyone else to do!"

Now she could hear him wrestling with the warmer-upper in the cooking room. The round iron rings made a noise. Ak! surely food was being prepared, and she hurried to call his attention and say she was finished.

"Please—here is your knife I have used. It happens now that one goes."

Bozi answered as she had expected: she must not go before she had eaten a little. Ivalu sat in the circle of women and looked at the papers with glass in front of them, which were hung up on the wall for people to look at. But Bozi took her arm and made her sit at the table where they were eating. It was a large wooden table, much larger than the side planks of a house, and completely smooth, like ice, so that one's hand could slide over it.

Ivalu had never eaten here before, but now she was a sewing woman, who had done a service. Tea was put on the table, and sugar, and many little pieces of bread that were also full of sweet. Every time that she and the others emptied their cups and plates, Bozi said it was not enough. Elias was the one who passed the food around.

Bozi's eyes laughed and he told of his joy for things that were warm and did not let one freeze, and then he suddenly asked Ivalu what she wanted in payment for sewing for Uzugodark. Ama had told him that she had been without sleep in the night in order to finish the things quickly and for this he wanted to give her something nice.

Ivalu became embarrassed and said she wished no payment. "Ak! I am only a miserable woman who has sewn, as is the custom of the people." But Bozi went out and came back with a pair of scissors. Ivalu took them and put them into her boot shaft. She said nothing, so that the envious women sitting near the wall could not laugh at her, and say when they got home, that she had spoken unbecoming words. She would have liked to take Bozi's hand as he did when he met someone, but she did not know whether it was the custom of his land to do that also out of joy over receiving presents, and so she did not do it.

Chapter Thirteen

IT WAS still storming the next day, but Bozi had said he wanted to start North. It was likely that the Fat-Cheeked would quickly revenge the murder of his brother, and it would be a shame for Bozi, if someone whom he had promised to protect were killed.

So he got up early, went to Uvdluriak's house, and called out the men.

"To journey is not impossible, although somewhat difficult," Uvdluriak said. "If you want to start, then we will go."

So they got ready. Uvdluriak and Apilak brought their sleds in front of Bozi's house, so they could start together. First they drank coffee, which warmed them through and through while they loaded the sleds, then the whips snapped over the heads of the dogs and they drove off quickly.

When they came to the other side of the fjord and turned to ride around the foothills, the snowstorm swept directly against their faces. Bozi felt the snow biting into his eyes and mouth, and at the wrist the fine snow forced its way into his mittens. He had little experience in the use of the whip, so that soon he was the last in line. The others disappeared ahead and it was difficult to follow them in the darkness and storm.

Now the storm rose to its full strength. It was almost impossible to breathe without turning one's head a little. Making headway was difficult, for, if Bozi didn't keep after the dogs, they immediately stopped and curled up. He shouted at them—and suddenly he felt ashamed of having thought himself wiser than Uvdluriak, who had warned him against making this journey.

Then the other sleds appeared in front of him. They had stopped, and when he reached them the men stood there, laughing at him.

"The weather is bad," Uvdluriak said. "The snowstorm is becoming a little difficult."

Bozi could see this for himself, but Uvdluriak said it as though it were great news, and as though one had to come this far to discover it.

"It may be difficult to continue," Uvdluriak said. So they decided to turn back and postpone the trip until the weather got better.

The dogs sensed that they were headed for rest and food again, and their happiness was great as they galloped over the beach and stopped in front of Bozi's house.

Elias came out to meet his master with a face that looked as though he were close to tears. He said that things were going badly. Minik had declared himself master and had opened the closet of fine food, taken out the bottles and started to drink as soon as Bozi had left. Bozi, when he heard this, ran into the house and saw that Elias had surely told the truth.

There sat Minik, with a bottle to his lips and a filled pitcher in front of him on the table. His eyes were fixed, and when he saw Bozi he only nodded and continued drinking. When he finally took the bottle away from his mouth, he said, only, that he was sick and had to give himself new strength. Bozi was very angry, and it was easily seen. He pulled Minik to his feet and kicked the chair aside. But the whiskey had made Minik's limbs soft. His tongue was the only thing that was still of any use to him. His legs crumpled and he fell on the floor and lay there, but his tongue was going and stopped only now and then, when he hiccoughed.

"You must help me," Bozi said. "It is better to carry him into the little room and let him sleep."

Bozi told the others to cover Minik with skins so that he would not freeze—but, as soon as he was well again, he would be ordered to leave.

The anger of a white man is felt far and so the house was quiet, although they had returned from a trip and there should be much laughter. In the evening Minik's box was carried into the house corridor and Bozi opened it. It contained a great many of Bozi's possessions, tobacco, knives and cartridges. When the others saw it, they told Bozi that when Minik used to come visiting at their houses, he had often brought food and tobacco. They were ashamed, now, to have taken it, but Bozi quickly told them it could never be said that they had done wrong. And it also came out that Minik had paid some of the women, who had visited him while their husbands were away for catch, with much of Bozi's property.

"It is regrettable," Merquzaq said, "that things were taken away which were forbidden. If you knew Peary's ship, you would see how he has his doors fixed. A bent iron stick, which at one end is widened into a hole, makes them so strong it is impossible to open them. That is how it ought to be when a man possesses as much as is in this house."

"I also know that arrangement," Bozi said, "and I possess some of those bent sticks. But it was pleasant to live in a place where no one took anything that did not belong to him. That is what I was told. But as Minik has been in the land of the white people, the shame is our shame, and is not yours."

"No," Uvdluriak said, "you are mistaken. We, too, know people who take things whose use is forbidden to them. But the wisdom of the ancients told us that stealing is permitted when one needs the stolen things. In that case the owner should feel happy to lose his property."

"But, what do you do when a man takes foxes from other people's traps? Does nothing happen to him?"

"Oh, yes," Uvdluriak said. "The unpleasant thing which happens is that it is told around in all the settlements, and people laugh when they hear his name."

Bozi said that anyone who is disloyal to those who believe in him was very unpleasant to him, and so, for what he had done, Minik must leave the settlement. At that moment the door opened, and Minik entered. He had vomited, and his face was smeared. His eyes were spotted with red and under his skin one could see no blood.

"Minik!" Bozi said angrily. "You drank until your senses left you and you did it in spite of the fact that it was forbidden! Possessions not belonging to you were found in your box! For this you must leave—and as soon as the weather gets better you will leave this settlement, also!"

Minik shouted in a loud voice and laughed hoarsely. He started to jump around and fling his arms wildly, and then he burst into a loud howl. Bozi said he had better go into his room and sleep, because there was still madness left in his body. Then Minik went out, and the people sat there in wonderment.

Bozi opened the door through which Minik had gone and they heard a frightened shout. "Minik is dead!" Bozi cried, and jumped back into the room. The others stepped into the door opening and looked in.

Minik lay on his back, with a knife sticking into his heart. Bozi's first scare had passed, and he called, "Come and help him—he is dying! We must save his life!"

They got hold of his shoulders and legs, and carried him into the big room where it was light and one could see. Bozi said, "Ak! I didn't mean it as bad as that. My words are always harder than my thoughts."

But then Torngé began to laugh and Samik laughed also. For the knife had made no wound in Minik's body. He had stuck it through one of the button-holes of his jacket.

The people laughed, and said that Minik had fooled them. But Bozi showed great anger and his words were hard. He told Minik that now there was enmity between them. His worry over Minik's death had turned to anger against the living. Minik saw that he had made himself ridiculous, and everybody laughed at him. But he tried to act as if he were possessed by a spirit. He began to dance and his song was to show that a spirit was speaking through his mouth:

> My great grandfather
> Ha-ja-ja-ja
> My great grandfather
> Ha-ja-ja-ja
> Has come to me.

My grandfather's spirit has come to me,
A great spirit has come to me,
And he proclaims illness if you harm me.
Ha-ja-ja-ja!

Merquzaq told Bozi he needn't be afraid of Minik's song, for it was without power. They all knew
Minik's grandfather and this wasn't his spirit song,
at all. Minik was unable to sing in the manner of
the people. He had forgotten how during his long
stay away from the land, and his melody was ridiculous and not right.

Bozi took Minik's arm and led him into the little
room which was at the end of the corridor. "Stay
here," he said, "and sleep till daylight. For then you
must travel—your stay in this house is ended."

When Bozi returned, he said that the happenings
had taken all joy from his senses, and therefore it was
best for everybody to go home. But he wanted to
speak to Merquzaq.

The old man's one eye lighted up like a blubber
torch, and he immediately became a man with whom
Bozi wished to discuss important things.

"Yes, it is best that you go," he said. "Go—so
that Bozi and I can talk to one another without having our talk disturbed by other unnecessary talk!"

And the people left.

"You see," Bozi said, "that Minik is a man who doesn't belong among the desirable ones."

"Yes, I have seen that he is not at all desirable," Merquzaq agreed.

"I was told that your granddaughter, Ivalu, was to become his wife!"

"Ak yes," Merquzaq said. "It is not impossible that this decision was made."

"Does she want to marry him?"

That Merquzaq did not know.

"Ivalu seems to be very capable," Bozi went on, "and I am very sorry for her. Don't let Minik become her husband. She deserves a better one."

Thoughts went through Merquzaq's head.

"Ivalu shall be brought here this very night," he said, and was immediately a man who procured a wife for Bozi, the white man.

"Ak, no," Bozi said. "I am not looking for a wife from this tribe. In the land from which I come a woman is waiting for me. But I had promised Minik they might both live here in my house, and my promise holds no longer. Let Ivalu stay in one place, and Minik in another."

When he returned home, Merquzaq told all this to Ivalu.

The next morning the storm had subsided and Bozi got up and went in to Minik, who was still asleep.

"Get up—you must travel!"

Minik began to wake up.

"You are not living here any longer," Bozi said. "Go to the north or the south. We have put provisions for your trip in the corridor, and you may take your things along. But only what belongs to you!"

A short while later dogs howled outside, and a sled drove away.

Chapter Fourteen

DARKNESS now spread over the people.

Bozi received visitors from the windward side, who brought many fox skins to trade for guns, knives and other implements. The women got needles and pots in which food could be cooked quickly, but always, after their trading was finished, there was one thing more they wanted but were ashamed to ask for. Presently Bozi realized that this was a mirror, in which they could look at themselves. Bozi was a man easy with his tongue, and he told them they were very wise to want mirrors for, when placed behind a lamp, the lamp was seen again in the mirror, and they had more light in their houses. To this the women said yes, that is what happens, and that that was why they wanted mirrors.

Bozi received many foxes, his pots cooked all day long, and everyone ate his fill. They drank much tea and coffee, and whenever the sleds left on a trip Bozi gave them a little of the kind of food which he ate, to take home, so they would not forget their visit too soon.

Then, one day, new sleds were seen approaching the settlement.

The moon was already small, and it was so dark one could scarcely see who was coming below on the ice. They were from a tribe which Bozi did not know.

"Joy, joy over the arrival!" shouted the men from below. One of the settlement replied: "Aye, in great measure, in great measure is there joy!"

"Ak! the journey was far and we longed to be here."

"Ak! was it far? Ak! were you longing?" shouted the men of the settlement again, and ran to meet them.

On the first sled sat a big, gay figure, and a little woman with a child on her back.

"Ak! I am so embarrassed," the man said.

"You should not be embarrassed!" Samik cried. "We are quite ordinary people."

It was evident that the visitors were very rich in meat. Huge lumps of frozen narwhal were handed off the sled and laid on the meat rack, and when they were finished piling it up, the rack looked like the house of a big catcher. That was what Bozi said to the others, and they laughed as they escorted the guest inside.

He was a big, heavy-set man with a huge round face full of smiles, from the corners of his eyes down to his chin. It was the Fat-Cheeked.

He said he had heard that Bozi greeted newcomers by getting hold of their hands, so he grabbed Bozi's right hand and laughed. When Bozi heard him called by name, he was surprised that this man could brew revenge, for it was a very happy man who came to visit.

Bozi had Elias prepare tasty food, and invited the Fat-Cheeked and his family to sleep in his house. They were very happy. "Now, at last, we have luck on our journey. Surely we will have a lot to tell when we return home!"

When Bozi had retired he began to think it was wrong to let a man who had sworn blood revenge against one of the settlement, stay in his house, for the people might think he liked such things. He decided to have a talk with the Fat-Cheeked the following morning.

He and his guests were drinking tea and eating meat the next day, when Apilak arrived. Bozi had sent for him.

"One found something important on the way," the Fat-Cheeked said to Apilak. "You lost your red dog, and it came to my sled, so I harnessed him with my own dogs. Ak! they were completely shamed to be seen in such imposing company. What a dog he is!"

When the Fat-Cheeked could find no more words of praise, Apilak answered him: "Ak! did he come to you? Yes, he ran away from me on the ice. He must be worse than ever, now, after being with your powerful, fast-running team!"

Bozi was astounded. Were these two really en-

emies? Were these really a murderer and a brother
of the murdered man, who stood talking in this
friendly manner, praising one another's dogs? Bozi
himself was a man who always spoke without preparing his listeners, or giving them time to prepare
an answer. He spoke that way now:

"One heard that a man was killed. One heard
it was Uvizakazek, and that *his* family has decided
to kill, also."

At this both men were silent. The Fat-Cheeked
took the smile from his eyes and his face became
hard.

"Now you speak of things which one does not
mention when many are present," he said.

Apilak said: "I did not think such words would
be spoken, so I am without an answer."

But Bozi continued, "Are you then not determined
to revenge Uvizakazek?"

"My brother has been killed and for that exchange
must be given," the Fat-Cheeked said, quietly.

But then Bozi said that, when a man is killed, his
children must go around in bad clothes and do not
have the happiness of other children, who have their
homes in the houses of trappers. And the man who
killed will himself be killed, and *his* children will
suffer, and so it would go on and on. "Think of your
children, and show that you are people who can

225

think. A man who is dead does not come back, even if the Fat-Cheeked will shoot one or two men!"

After he spoke, they were silent for a long time. Apilak was the first to think about his words, and he agreed with Bozi. He felt like crying, he said, when he thought that his little children might starve and have no warm clothes in the winter.

The Fat-Cheeked opened his eyes and then closed them again.

"It seems that new times have come into our land. White men are masters over us miserable people, and, therefore, it is best to keep out of the way of their anger. But my poor brother is dead. And he had a gun which has been lost and his meat has been eaten by fellow settlers."

"I will give you a gun," Bozi said, quickly, "and many boxes of cartridges. As compensation for the meat, I shall give you tea and sugar. And you may take knives and axes and wood for a sled, if you will not fight with those who have killed your brother."

"Can I talk back to a white man?" asked the Fat-Cheeked. "When you wish something, I am forced to do your will. Maybe it is only forgetfulness on your part that you did not also include a pipe and tobacco for me."

"Yes, I forgot that you smoke," Bozi said. "You shall have them, too."

"It is good that now one can begin to laugh again,"

the Fat-Cheeked said. "It is best to speak of other things. Then it cannot be said that we are in a bad mood, and spend our visit in speaking of a man who is dead." And he laughed.

Bozi offered tea, and while they were drinking he brought the things which he had promised to his visitor.

"Ak! this is all too fine," said the Fat-Cheeked. He smiled at the gun, looked through the barrel, and felt all its parts.

He was given a knife and a saw, and, when he received a hatchet, he exclaimed over it and said that now he was a different man from what he had been. "Now one wishes tobacco again," he laughed. Bozi gave him many pieces, and a pipe and matches.

"This is the last time you will see me," the Fat-Cheeked said. "For I am not altogether without shame. Just think, if you also gave my wife needles, I would be forced to flee to the far north to hide my face!"

His wife got needles and thread rolled around pieces of wood which were narrow in the middle. Yes, and many things of which one never even thought!

"It is good," exclaimed the big man, "that you have not offered her a mirror. I had forbidden her to accept one."

So the woman got a mirror.

"Ak!" the Fat-Cheeked said, "let me go from here quickly. I am completely ashamed that I can give you nothing for thanks. If only I were a trapper with a sense of honor!" He got up and brought in two seal skin sacks.

"Just look how impudent!" the woman said. "He is bringing his miserable fox skins."

"Quiet there in the corner!" the Fat-Cheeked said to her. "Are women talking, too? Did I say I want to give them to him? Ak! I only wish to help the white man a little when he washes his shiny floors. In case he wants to dry them, here are a few useless skins which should not be unpacked until there is no one present. For our shame must not be known."

Bozi took the sacks and opened them. They contained wonderful skins, dark and light blue foxes, rich compensation for the goods the Fat-Cheeked had received. Bozi took a few of them and asked his visitor what he wanted in exchange.

"Nothing," he said. "Have I not received presents from you?"

"But that was to make peace in the land, and to end all enmities."

"Ak! I am not a man who can steal," the Fat-Cheeked said. "I have never accepted gifts without giving a small compensation. A poor man like me cannot offer more than this. I am a bad trapper and my wife does not know the art of preparing skins."

Those were the words of the Fat-Cheeked. The next day he left, and Apilak went with him. Old Merquzaq said to Bozi that happiness reigned among them, and that Zigdlu in the north was safe.

More and more people came to trade, and then went back to their homes. Bozi sat at home day after day, waiting for the visitors' foxes, and he had many to hang in his storeroom. Elias took charge of them and the people got more desire to sell skins when they saw how carefully Bozi handled them.

At times he went for catch with the others, and Merquzaq taught him how to be shrewd against the foxes and lure them into his traps. One night, on one of these trips, they slept in a big mountain cave. Merquzaq told him tales. He told how Samik's father, in an attack of madness, had cut open his own stomach and had died from the wound after he again became conscious. And he told Bozi about the time Uvdluriak's little son had been shot through the heart as the result of a medicine man's curses. And Bozi heard many things which showed him that the people were unusual, and had not only happiness living in their thoughts nor only gay words on their tongues.

Bozi got out a sleeping-bag and reindeer skins to sleep on. "Have you nothing to keep you warm?" he asked Merquzaq.

"I belong to a time when sleeping-bags were not used," the old man said. "And I was already grown up when the white man came to the land and introduced new customs. I had learned nothing about sleeping-bags and tobacco."

"Don't you want to borrow some of mine?"

But Merquzaq said the protection of the cave was enough.

"I am old and full of thoughts. It does no harm if I stay without sleep for a while. On hunting trips I have always thought about the prey, not of sleep. Besides, tonight we have taken a lot of nourishment that is like an inner cushion which bears warmth."

Bozi woke up to the stare of Merquzaq's one eye, which bored into his brain like an awl. They got up and Bozi made tea.

"Men cook much better than women," the old man said.

But Bozi said he was longing for food prepared by a woman, and hoped that soon a woman would come to his house. Merquzaq said the people were wondering that he had so far refused the women of the tribe, and that they were not used to this from white men.

"But would you like it," Bozi asked, "if I should, for instance, take your little granddaughter, Ivalu?"

Merquzaq looked at him in amazement.

"Is she not a woman? She was married once, and her husband was killed. Now she mourns that she is alone. Should I, her grandfather, not wish her that which a woman needs?"

"Yes, but you should see that the man she gets will make her a good husband. You surely would not like it if she were to take one man today and another tomorrow, and not be properly married to one?"

"Why has the white man such thoughts, when he makes no attempts to take her? We miserable people up here feel contempt for him who lies. But our bodies and our passions speak their language in us, and the body does not lie. Him one must obey."

They rode home from the cave and on the way stopped and looked at their traps.

"Because one has been created a man, and has become an inhabitant of the world, one must conquer prey," Merquzaq said, and he muttered powerful words, which were to lure foxes into his traps. Bozi wanted to learn those words, but Merquzaq said it was impossible.

"Words which have gained power through the wisdom of the fathers should not be needlessly repeated and so made weak," said the old man. "But I can help you set your traps, and perhaps your wise knowledge can create a substitute for the well-meaning spirits of the hunt."

Toward the South lived many people. They had peculiar houses and caught animals in a different way from the people of the north. They were full of knowledge of other things, too, for each year ships came and brought them white men's products in large quantities. Never were their enormous warehouses empty of provisions.

Bozi decided to journey to these people to inquire about conditions in his own land.

"This shows," Merquzaq said, "that he thinks of that which he has left behind. And it means that his pleasure over this place has not completely swallowed him." Many of them thought that Bozi had only been here on a visit, and was now going to leave.

He went to Uvdluriak and Torngé, and asked them to go with him. Uvdluriak did not want to say no, as adventure was to be expected. Torngé was also ready.

One day, while many of the people sat in his house preparing dog harness for the journey, Bozi began to speak of his plans. A white man does not know enough to fear speaking about himself. He will even mention the names of others, although they may be far away and sick, with their souls feeble and unable to stand being called into the presence of others.

Bozi said that in the south he would receive a paper on which the fate of his family would be marked. He said, too, that a woman for whose lonesomeness he felt sorry would also have marked down her decision about a journey to Bozi the next year.

Again the men had to look at each other, for it was indeed peculiar that a man, in the presence of others, would speak of a woman and so show himself to be weak.

"Let us lend him our women so his yearning may be satisfied," they said. But Bozi acted as though these words aroused anger in him. So the visitors used their mouths only to chew dog harness, which is, after all, more useful than talk—which is only for people to listen to, and nothing else.

Torngé was the biggest man of the tribe and a fast dog driver. Uvdluriak was a master trapper, who owned the fastest dog team. So Bozi could not have chosen better companions. Meat was brought from the stone pits—large pieces of walrus skin, which could lie flat on the sled and prevent the cross pieces from breaking in the thawing snow; wonderful, crisply rotted narwhal meat with lamp blubber on it; whale skin for the people, and meat for the dogs. Bozi himself took all sorts of food in closed iron containers, and tea for every evening, so that everyone in the settlement wished they could go along.

Before their departure, Bozi gathered all the settlers together for a joint meal. Kazaluk was leaving the feast earlier than the others, to go home and sew the remaining clothes. She went to Bozi before she left.

"One goes home," she said, "and one wishes you all a fast trip and much catch."

"Thank you," Bozi answered. "If you wish something from down there, just tell me."

"Does one not have everything one wishes?" Kazaluk answered. "But there is something for which I should like to ask, if my tongue were not so scared."

"What is it you wish for?"

"Ak! it is not a wish. But I have heard there are many women there and that they are beautiful. And now it is my husband with whom you are to journey . . ."

Bozi jumped up and his talk was fast.

"Ak!" he exclaimed. "Are women in all lands not alike? They do not trust their husbands and are always full of fear of losing them. I come from a country where women are like that, but I thought that in this land you are different, and less difficult."

Kazaluk was completely ashamed.

"I did not wish to arouse regrettable memories in you," she said. "I was only thinking of my husband."

"Yes," Bozi said. "That is just it. Can he not look out for himself? Why don't you come to an agreement between yourselves whether you want to be true to each other on journeys or not?"

"Ak! Now my talk is without meaning to you," Kazaluk said. I did not wish to make you angry

I only meant to say I have heard of the many women and my husband is so alone. Should a woman come up to his taste, wouldn't you then be a little helpful to him?"

At this Bozi began to laugh and the others all laughed. Kazaluk looked at them, not knowing what their laughter was about. Bozi held her hand tight and said yes, he would look out for her husband, and that he would bring her a present from their journey to the south.

Elias was a man who could also write on paper. He gave Bozi words which he put into flat bags, and all looked on with much awe. After the three men had left, Elias remained behind, and was a master who invited people to drink tea in his house, and spoke a little louder than when his own master was present.

In Cape York Bozi stopped with Mayark, who received him well. His throat widened and he tasted all sorts of good things. They brought in a large sealskin filled with little auks which had been potted in the blubber. They were frozen and had to be broken apart with a hatchet and, while eating them, one could get feathers in one's mouth as well as bird meat.

Mayark put one side of the bed plank at Bozi's disposal, but it was late before he could taste sleep. A young woman had come in. She was a quiet girl, with no beauty in her face, and was cross-eyed and did not smile.

"Ak! she is embarrassed," Mayark said. "One finds you are to be felt sorry for in your loneliness. See—here is a woman to keep you company in the night. Now it is time to retire."

They began to undress.

"See how her breasts swell," Mayark said. "Ak! It makes me turn to my old wife and think. You ought to take a woman along with you. Perhaps you will be pleased with her, and will reward me later."

But Bozi was tired and deaf to his talk. He rolled himself into the covers, but something was disturbing his sleep. He lifted his head. By the half light in the house, which came from the small flame of the lowered lamp, he saw the girl lying near him. She was wide awake. One eye was turned toward him and the other toward the ceiling. He thought for a moment, but for only a short moment. Then he rolled himself into his covers again, having made a definite decision.

The next time he noticed he was alive everybody in the house was up and dressed. It was already so late in the day that light showed in the south. And a big feast was to begin in the next house. The man had brought the best that people could eat: dried meat, potted in blubber, was the choicest food, and there is no one alive who does not give up talking when there is *orzut* to eat.

It was prepared in the summer with much care. First a narwhal was caught. Then the women dried it on both sides, in the sun, so that it became black and enticing for the mouths of the people. A second narwhal was skinned so that the blubber remained on the hide, and this blubber was cut into pieces the size of one's hand. These pieces and the dried meat were stuffed into a catch bladder, and pressed under rocks until the blubber had become oil, and had taken on the strong taste which causes guests at a meal to be silent.

Now they all came into the house of the trapper. At the idea of the delicious food they were to get they found their mouths watering, and it was difficult to look empty of thought and to speak of indifferent things. But Mayark had still another surprise in store. Ak! it was altogether unsuspected. No one knew he had prepared walrus liver during the summer. It was green with strength, and burned the palate like the black powder which Bozi put on meat.

And there was even one more thing, the big event of the feast. Those outside in the corridor shouted, "Listen, you in there! Take the end of this miserable catch belt and pull into the house what we have out here! Help us!"

Those inside pulled with all their strength. They dragged and groaned. This was an enormous morsel, and something which they had never seen before. They could not move it, and several of them proposed to give up, and cut it in pieces outside. In the corridor, Mayark shouted that he was ashamed to bring in what was to be served now. Finally, Bozi, ignorant of the customs for visitors in this country, grabbed forcefully at the belt and pulled the whole thing in a little sooner than it was supposed to be, and everybody laughed very much.

It was a whole seal, stuffed with things and frozen. The host took an axe, cut a hole in the seal's skin, and stuck his hand into the frozen walrus oil, which was white and thick from the cold. He got hold of a few pieces of dried meat and whale skin, and began to eat.

"Have it taken out right away," he said. "That which I wanted to offer you has turned out completely bad. It is mixed with dog dirt and bad things. It is terrible—everything is spoiled."

"Nau! Nau!" he continued, and took another piece of whale skin. The others had no more strength with which to resist any longer, and reached in, too. Everybody dug into the wonderful sack. The oil from their hands was dripped into the lamps, and some of it was poured into the blubber pail. But everything solid was eaten.

Mayark's wife, who was sitting on the bed plank with the other women, was handed a piece. They had all taken off their boots, and were shouting for dried meat and whaleskin, wanting more and more. Then they became quiet. And nothing pleases a host more than having his guests quiet and peaceful at a meal. Their smacking and sucking was to his ears pleasant as sleep.

But soon the women had really had enough, and were only eating for their own amusement. They began to talk between every bite, praising the hospitality, remembering other feasts, and soon the whole house was filled with women's talk. Mayark was a little embarrassed at their behavior, and lifted his head and listened. Then he shouted, "How? Has spring come while we were eating? The auks must have come, and we must be living under a bird hill, listening to the chatter of bird beaks, so that men are made silent by the noise!"

The women were ashamed, and were silent. But soon after, they were again whispering. For the pleasure of eating was over for them, and they could not suppress their voices.

Chapter Fifteen

FURTHER and further South they travelled. A journey over immeasurable country in the darkness is a difficult task; the dogs get thin and the daily treks seem endless.

Bozi learned much. He was becoming a man who could journey and reach his destination, alone.

They slept under the open sky, lying in sleeping-bags with a sealskin spread over their heads, until the cold would seize them. Then it would force them to lie there, rubbing their feet together, and forgetting sleep.

Bozi noticed that he had lice and complained to the others about it, but they only laughed. Was his country without lice, like the people here a long, long time ago? Then even water would burn, but now everything that lives has lice, the birds in the air and the seals in the water. "If you did not have them until now, then it is a sign that you are beginning really to belong to this land. For now the lice find you good-tasting!"

That evening they made camp behind an iceberg, which pushed itself against the wind, like a dam. They lighted a blubber fire, a tiny spot, which made everything around still blacker in the winter night. It became the only thing in the world.

From the fissures by the iceberg, they took out the

new ice and sank their walrus hides into the water, to thaw them out while they ate. Bozi cut up a walrus skin without first having scraped off the salt which clung to it after soaking. Neither of the others said anything about it until he started to feed it to the dogs. Then they told him that his dogs would die, or at least get very sick, from the salt.

"Why didn't you tell me before I cut it up?" Bozi asked. "Now it will be frozen again before I can finish scraping it!"

"How could a miserable person tell a white man what to do?" asked Uvdluriak.

"No—we are without speech with you, but we speak of your dogs out of pity," Torngé said.

Bozi got angry and, when they offered to help him prepare his dog food, he said he would do it alone. While he ate, his face was without a smile, and he quickly lay down in his sleeping-bag without saying a word to either of them. Then they whispered, out of fear of his anger: ' Ak! we have made him un-friendly, and perhaps from now on he is an enemy. Perhaps that will bring dissension into our camp. It is not impossible that we should kill him in order to secure peace, and then return home."

It was Torngé who said this. But Uvdluriak thought it would be enough, now that he was asleep, only to remove his gun. Should his face still be without friendliness in the morning, then perhaps the right thing would be to kill him.

"It is remarkable that he should feel anger against us, who were only modest, and did not want to prevent him from cutting up his walrus hide as he wanted to. But we are a miserable people and know nothing of a stranger!"

Next morning Bozi awoke early and was freezing. While he put on his fur coat, and his head was still in the frozen cowl, he jumped around and stamped his feet. While doing this, he fell, because of the unevenness of the ice. He laughed at his own clumsiness and his laughter awakened the others. They saw that Bozi had slept and forgotten his anger, and it was possible for them to be friendly and glad, also. Now, no murder was necessary. The killing would have made them very sad, anyway, as they liked the white man, and he had never before given them grounds for very much fear.

The period of deep darkness was over, and in the day time one could see the color of the dogs, and could even catch glimpses of icebergs which were far in the distance. The ice was easily passable and they could sit on the sleds for long stretches, but when the moon rose, it became hard for Bozi to keep pace with his companions. Moonlight behind throws no shadows to mark the unevenness in the ice and, if one is not experienced in driving a dog team, one cannot avoid a fall.

They were lying on their sleds and sleeping, when a bear came near their camp! The dogs jumped up, and their disturbance awoke the men. Torngé and Uvdluriak were on their feet immediately, and the dogs took their places, almost harnessing themselves for the chase. The sleeping-bags and other things were quickly rolled up, and two of the sleds were off. Only Bozi still stood there, and his dogs howled in eager fury. As the white man untied the sled the animals leaped forward. There was a jolt, and he sprawled on his face. The darkness swallowed the dogs, and with his gun in his hand Bozi rushed into the blackness after them.

Uvdluriak was ahead. His dogs put their heads up, let their hind legs kick skyward, and swept by the big Torngé. The bear was fleeing from them, but on smooth ice his speed was too slow, and soon they heard him waddling along, quite close.

One dog was cut loose, and then another. They disappeared up ahead, and their teammates howled angrily after the lucky ones, increasing their speed so that the men had to jump on the crossbars of the sleds.

There was a great yelping out in front as the dogs overtook their quarry and leapt on it from behind. Again a dog was cut loose—and still another. Ak!

now the animal was done for. It is impossible to flee with a team of dogs behind, or even two dogs, with many teeth which bite securely. Soon the hunters overtook the thrashing, growling animals, and killed the bear.

As soon as the animal is killed, everything becomes quiet. The dogs lose their fierceness and hatred. Some lie down, and others go over, licking the wounds of the dead bear and lapping up a little blood.

As they all stood there, Bozi's dogs shot by. They came all bunched together, for their harness had gotten twisted. They stormed straight at the dead animal and wanted to attack the lifeless prey. This disturbed the peace of the other dogs and a fight started. Finally, with shouts and beatings on the part of the men, howlings and whinings on the part of the dogs, the animals were straightened out. Uvdluriak used his spear shaft and Torngé broke his whip before they could get them apart.

The bear was already skinned and they were getting ready to cut the meat up for food by the time Bozi came running. He breathed fast and the cold frost stood around his mouth.

"Did you get the bear?" he asked, but, at the same moment, he saw what was lying there.

"We couldn't wait until you got here," the men said, regretfully. "Our dogs were in danger during the battle." But Bozi smiled and said he was pleased with the idea of fresh-cooked meat, and grateful for the experience he had had.

The two trappers put the pelt on their sleds, and fed the dogs with the wonderful, fresh, soft meat, and it was as if summer had come into their stomachs.

Bozi had come away without his outer fur coat. The wind was biting his head and cutting through his jacket, and his body could not give enough resistance. The others noticed it and became worried.

"We must help our companion," they said, and ran quickly for the camp, trying to keep Bozi warm.

"Jump off the sled and run," Torngé shouted to him, but when Bozi tried it his legs were without strength. They rubbed his sides without his being able to feel it, and when they finally arrived Uvdluriak decided to build a snow house. In the meanwhile Torngé did everything he could to keep Bozi from falling asleep.

"It is going to storm," Uvdluriak said, when the hut was finished. "It is best to ice it immediately."

They had already started to throw in their things, but now they had to take them out again. Bozi was cold all through by now, and had no desire except to get into the house, to warmth and sleep.

"Why do you throw the skins out again? I can feel that the frost has caught me. Let me go in!"

But they continued to throw everything out in

a heap, and Bozi thought he had to get angry to get his will. But it did not help him a bit.

"I want to go in—do you hear? I am freezing to death!"

He thought that the cold had gotten him more than it really had. That is the way it feels to the inexperienced.

Inside, Uvdluriak made fire with blubber and turf, so that the whole snow house shone like the sun. Then he crawled out and closed the entrance with a snow block. He filled in all the cracks; the thought he had was to let no heat come out. For when one takes the fire away afterwards, the thawed snow on the walls freezes to ice, and the house can laugh at the storm.

Bozi, however, thought they were planning to kill him, and his thoughts became wild. He shouted strange words, without sense, and it was difficult to keep him away from the house.

"Ak! you want my death!" he shouted. "Let me live! Why did you carry me this far, and not kill me sooner?"

They could see he was speaking without knowing what he said, and they carried him into the house. Here it was wonderful and warm, and his thoughts soon quieted. When his skins and sleeping-bag were brought in, they helped him get off his frozen things and crawl into the warm reindeer skins. Soon he knew nothing of what was happening and did not even hear the howling snowstorm.

When he awoke the blubber lamp was burning and the tea pot hung over the fire. The door was walled in and only the noise of the raging storm came through the walls. The house was strong. Uvdluriak told him they had to laugh at his eagerness in trying to get into it. A man does not die of cold until his eyes are frozen in his head, and as long as one can walk straight and talk, there is no danger. They explained to him why they had not let him get into the house right away. Bozi said he was ashamed of his thoughts, but Torngé laughed. Shortly they were all laughing and talking in the house, while outside the wind was sweeping the snow over the dogs and sleds.

At last they arrived. The houses reached from the beach far back into the land. A white man in a very thick jacket met them, very representative and important. He stretched his arms in many directions, and wherever he pointed, people hurried about. The white women came out, seized Bozi by the hand, and shook his arm. Then they all went into the big house. It was filled with a fragrance, as if reindeer tallow was being melted, and the smell caused Bozi and his companions to become mightily hungry. Soon they got more than enough to eat, the daughter of the house filling their plates again and again. At last, after many lean days, they could make their throats happy by belching, which is as it should be after a feast.

Later there was great joy in the house. Many friends from the settlement came, shouting and laughing, and shortly they all started running around the room. Without shame each took the woman he favored most, and swung her around while he ran. Often they changed the women among themselves, and they were all delighted. The heat in the house became oppressive, but the people continued this restless manner of relations. Now and then two women, out of anger that no man chose them, began to run around with one another. The result was always that a few men were sorry for them and also ran with them.

But otherwise, there was so much confusion that the two strangers could not observe everything. They waited only for the lamps to be put out. They thought, then, to abandon their embarrassment and seize women for themselves. Torngé said to Uvdluriak that one could now see the great foresight of the southlanders, since the running around and jumping must be aimed at making the women warm-blooded and fiery for love, when the time should come.

They sat there, tense, and thought only that they were waiting too long for the signal of putting out the lamps. The host himself did not run around the room. He sat in the innermost room and had a bottle in front of him from which he drank in quite small portions. Now and again he went to the others, for he had a little drinking cup in his hand and he poured for various others whom he wanted to distinguish. Those who did not get any from him turned their heads longingly after him. Torngé and Uvdluriak got none, as the man said the drink was too strong for their gullets.

The people continued to run around and the heat became almost too much to be pleasant. Still nobody undressed, but ran around and shouted and turned in circles, so that it was difficult for the two from the north to keep an eye on the women they had picked for themselves. But finally the host made a sign with his hand. The time had come! and Torngé and Uvdluriak got up to be prepared for the big event.

But the light was not turned out. The people only laughed and were shouting that the evening had been very amusing—and then they all went home.

They are going to continue in another house, Uvdluriak thought, and made for the door. He saw that the gaiety and excitement had left them all. They stopped and talked about the Northern Lights, saying that they were shining brightly, and that the threatening weather had stayed away after all.

Torngé and Uvdluriak were disappointed and embarrassed. As all the visitors began to walk slowly in different directions, it was clear to them that love in this land was without battle, and that it was not introduced with a wrestling match through which one contested for certain women.

"He who travels experiences new customs," Uvdluriak said to Torngé. "But it is cold, and now, surely, we should go to sleep."

So then they went into the big house and it was sleeping time. Bozi and the two men were to sleep on the floor in one room by themselves, but Torngé and Uvdluriak were too astounded by the new things they had seen to be able to sleep.

Bozi took a great many small flat bags with writing on them. He said he had waited to look at these words which had been sent to him, until he would not be disturbed. He looked among them until he found one whose lines of writing were known to him. And then he forgot the presence of the two men.

They looked at him, thinking it was too bad that all the things they could learn had to be spoken to them through their ears. But their eyes were not practiced in making out thoughts which were on paper. Suddenly they saw that Bozi's face was changing.

He said something that was neither words nor crying, but one could understand that the happiness in him had disappeared. His eyes were without motion and without sight. That was how medicine men looked when they went on their spirit journeys, and were not in possession of their senses.

For a long time he remained motionless, his hands closed around the paper which was crumpled between his fingers.

"It is different from what was expected—that we can see from your face," Uvdluriak said. "If you have forgotten to bring something on the sled, perhaps we can help you."

"Nothing has been forgotten. The being for whom I longed, and on whom I have thought, has written bad words."

"Ak! when friendship breaks, it becomes a difficult feud."

"It is not a man," Bozi said. "It is my beloved, in my country, she for whom I have waited and to whom I have spoken all my thoughts. Now she has written that she has met another. She was good to him and gave him everything."

After some time had passed, Uvdluriak said there was nothing to do but for Bozi to return to his home immediately and give his wife a thorough beating, so that his soul should come to peace. The effect of a woman's faithlessness is always hurtful, because one knows that the other man is laughing about one. Unfortunately one cannot take one's anger on him, for then it could be said that one is embarrassed because of a woman, and is dependent on her feelings.

"This is something much stronger than you could understand," Bozi said. "I will not return to my homeland and beat anybody. This woman was the only woman for me, and she had no equal. She is not one whom one can take—she is one who gives herself as a gift. But now she is lost."

Bozi continued to speak about her for a long time. He said that he felt neither sorrow nor happiness, but only that he could not understand how he had gone so far away, leaving her without a protector.

Torngé said that only the young and inexperienced believe that the woman whom they want is without fault. Even though one has been used to the sewing of one woman, one can surely become reconciled to another, even if one's boots change their form a little.

"Did you never want a woman you could not get?" Bozi asked Torngé.

"Yes. You are right," the big man answered. "That I have tried, and then I was more unhappy than in all my life."

Now it was he who sat there with quiet eyes, and thought.

"What did you do then?" Bozi asked, wanting to know the experience of other men.

"Yes, at first I was unhappy because a man who was stronger than I and whom I feared, had taken her. Later I became desirous of others, but that was because I was afraid people would discover my dependence on this particular woman, and laugh at me for it."

Early in the morning Bozi woke up and woke everybody in the house. He had evidently read more in the letters and had gotten new thoughts, for he asked the host how quickly he could get back to Umanak. Shortly he left the house, took the road which led over the hill, and examined the ice. His companions talked to one another about their own journey home. Their stomachs were filled with good-tasting things, and who can use his thoughts at such a time?

While they were still sitting and talking, the door opened and Bozi came in. His face was entirely different from what it always was, and his voice, too, sounded peculiar. He turned to his companions and said they should prepare everything for an immediate return and then come to the house where there was trading with the white man. There they could get everything they wanted to take back home with them.

The trading house was very big. The white owner of all these treasures stood behind a long table and asked them what they wanted. Who can bring his tongue to be impudent and immodest in such a case? They both said they were without wishes, that they pitied their dogs, and would not make them drag home more weight than they already must.

"Don't you want some coffee?" asked the merchant.

Yes, coffee was one of the things they would like to have. So they received coffee, sugar and bread. Then they got up again.

"Do you want a knife?"

"Yes. It so happens that we need knives very badly," they said. And the man gave them each a knife but such small ones that the children might use them for toys. Slowly Torngé got more courage. He looked up at the ceiling from which kettles were hanging. "It is not impossible that it would bring some happiness into my home, if I got one like those."

"Well, yes," the man said, and he climbed on a box and took down a kettle.

Torngé looked it over and turned it around in his hand.

"Isn't it a beautiful kettle?" the white man asked.

"I, too, wish to acquire a kettle," Uvdluriak said. But now the white man got impatient, and said that he should have been told this while he was standing on the box, and was stretching himself.

Then both thought that this must be a very great master, this man who placed no value in climbing on boxes and taking down kettles. That discouraged

Torngé so much that he said it was best if they went now, and received no more presents. But the white man reminded them that they should have tobacco and matches, and gave some to both men.

Bozi was busy getting his sled ready for the trip. He was quiet and his face was without a smile. It was clear that the letters could contain great power, and that he was badly hurt. So maybe it was a good fortune not to be able to interpret writing!

Chapter Sixteen

THE homeward journey was different from the one which they had made to the south, and different from any in the experience of Torngé and Uvdluriak. For in the evenings Bozi did not speak to them at all; but he was without anger and no complaint was heard from him.

One day they came to an iceberg which stood higher than any other in the vicinity, and as they were about to pass by they discovered a bear sticking its head over the edge, quite high up. Bozi was the one who shouted, and the others understood that he was again becoming a man who sees and hears, and does not just think. Grief's teeth are quickly worn down—and, after a while, grief itself does not bite any more.

Quickly they raced the sleds to the iceberg. There were no tracks to be seen, so they climbed up the sides very carefully. As the bear rushed them, they shot off their rifles, but in their fright they slid back to the ground, and lay at the foot of the berg, laughing heartily. Bozi laughed too, and even in the excitement Uvdluriak noticed it. But Torngé, who always worried whether the catch shares would be big enough, thought only of the bear.

They were quickly on their feet again, for the bear, wounded and bleeding, rushed down the berg at them in pain and fury. One shot finished him.

They had to climb up in order to get him and as they climbed higher, they became more worried. They had to support one another from behind, so that they could hold on to the treacherous surface of the ice.

Then a second bear appeared, a smaller one, but furious and growling, slapping at them with its paws. Uvdluriak, the first one to raise himself over the edge of the berg, got his gun up and killed it with one explosion.

These were evidently a little man and wife, living up here in a cave in the iceberg. One could tell, by the fact that there were no tracks down below, that they had not been down there for a long time. Now one of them lay on the ice where Uvdluriak had shot her; the other was deep in a depression and was hard to get out. They had to pull dogs up in order to have their help in getting him.

"This is good catch," Torngé said, still thinking of his share. "Two bears, which we have killed in mating time, and now they will be food for us and our dogs!"

Bozi said it would be more practical to dress the animals up there on the iceberg. Torngé and Uvdluriak said nothing. This contradicted what one had always been taught, but, if the white man said so, two miserable people really could not talk against it.

So they cut open the belly of the bigger one, a fat little man bear with a thick layer of fat. The guts gushed out, tangled and knotted. The stomach was empty, and evidently the two bears had just wanted to be a couple together, without hunger or nourishment. But the liver was sweet and large, and the blood streamed, hot and steaming, out into the clear frosty air. People sniff with happy noses when blood steams —and now it streamed, like a little river of life and strength, through the snow and down to the ice. It left only a small red stain on the snow as it sank through.

Now the pieces of meat were cut out. The hams were hard to cut loose, and Torngé stuck his knife between the vertebrae to part them from the torso. Bozi and Uvdluriak were bending over the other bear, whose turn came now.

And then it happened!

They heard only a crashing, rumbling noise, and everything under them became alive. The iceberg trembled, moved, and fell—and they had the feeling of being struck by a snowstorm packed into one solid mass. Bozi saw Torngé disappear downward, and in the same second he was gone. Uvdluriak could not see either of the others at all. His ears were filled with noise, which took the power from his eyes and killed his thoughts.

It was the iceberg revenging itself on them for letting blood run over it! Ak! one knew it was forbidden to have blood run on the sweet ice which breaks off the edge of the glaciers. The inland ice, lying beyond the fjords, watches carefully that the land shall not be sullied by the people. It is the same with ice-bergs, which find the doings of people offensive. The ice must not feel any blood on itself. Yes, it often does not take even that much to offend the white, over-powering mountains! But Bozi was a white man and often laughed at their fear of nature—that was why they guessed his power was not smaller than that of an ordinary iceberg.

But now they saw the truth! The blood had pene-trated through the snow layer and had tickled the body of the ice. It had burst with anger. Yes, and it did not burst into two pieces, like a stone, for the ice was more manifold than stone. Nobody living knows everything about the ice. The iceberg became many icebergs. It bursts into great pieces and then all these pieces burst into smaller ones. The thunder did not stop, and Uvdluriak thought, "It must be like this when one is murdered and shot in the brain and gets death into oneself!"

He remembered how he had shot to death the medicine man, Kajurak. The murdered man's face and eyes had expressed these same feelings before he stopped breathing. Now Uvdluriak felt them, and he could not pull himself together and look around, for before he had absorbed one peal of thunder, another came from the other side. Ice was everywhere, and thoughts came to him again only when he found himself sitting wedged tightly in a crevice. When he tried to lift his leg, he felt in it only pain and weakness.

Bozi fell. How, or how deep, he did not know. Suddenly he was in the water, but at the same moment there came up from underneath a horrible mountain of ice, which flung him high in the air, and he landed face downward. He could not think of anything except that it was good that he had his fur cowl, or his head would have been dashed to pieces.

The terrible noise continued. He wanted to run, but all around him floated pieces of ice like the one he was on, and he could not get anywhere. He did not think to look around him, he ran to the edge of the huge piece on which he was riding alone. Suddenly he was hit on the back and hurled over to solid ice, but there he lay without knowing where he had fallen.

And still the terrible noise continued. None of the three was aware of himself or saw either of the others. Bursts of sound, crashings and plungings of the heaving ice came in too many numbers to let fear reach them. For to have fear, one must be able to take hold of it.

Bozi then realized he was on solid ice again and, without thought, he got up and ran as fast as he could. He could again notice that he was a man. He saw that the iceberg was gone—but in its place was another one, smaller, but wider and of quite a different shape. It was still heaving and throwing off big blocks which broke holes in the ice under foot.

Bozi was dripping with water, but fright was calling inside him, calling louder than the cold. He heard a shout, "Nau! Nau!" come over the ice, and this brought him back to his senses.

It was growing dark again after the short twilight, and he could not see the caller clearly.

"Nau! Nau!" the shout came again. "Are there people alive here?"

It was Uvdluriak. Bozi answered, they called back and forth a few times, and then they were again together. Uvdluriak saw immediately that Bozi had been in the water and saw the fright on his face. He, himself, was full of pain in his leg. From the moment that he had been caught tightly until the ice shifted and freed him, he had fought to remain alive—but how, he did not know! It was as though he had been wrestling with nature itself. But still he had escaped, and now he was here.

They both laughed and grasped each other's hands. Then they turned toward the place where the struggle had taken place and caught sight of Torngé.

He stood quite calmly by the sled, and was going about picking up things and placing them together as though something quite usual had happened.

As the iceberg began to turn upside down he had jumped off and at the same time had been thrown clear. He heard the crashing behind him, and suddenly saw the dogs which they had taken up on the berg thrown into the air and crushed to pieces by the falling ice.

"The iceberg surely must have noticed that I advised against dressing the bears up there," he said. "An iceberg protects a man who honors it. Now I am only collecting these things, here!"

The journey was difficult with only the few dogs which had been saved, but young men always have the will to live, and he who does not wish to die can stand strenuous effort. So they pushed on and on, and finally Torngé, who was in the lead, shouted back to the others and pointed. They came up and saw sled tracks in the snow.

A sled track is like a white man's book, and from it one can see who has journeyed and what has happened. The sign of a whip in the snow is known, and the tracks of the dogs can tell everything about a journey. Here the snow was stamped solid and quite dirty from the steps of people, and at last they saw a light in a window. It shone out into the darkness, and to them it was like a seal which bobs up in a still,

desolate fjord after a hungry man has waited in vain
for a whole day. It was like the talk of a mother to
tired children. Ak! to Bozi it was as if someone had
given him water on a mountain hike, on a hot summer
day. They all stood still a little while and gazed toward
it. Then they ran to overtake their sled and, as they
caught it again, their thoughts were full of joy.

Before they themselves could shout, they were discovered from the land. A shouting of the children
told those in the houses that something was coming
over the ice. Immediately the people rushed out and
the place became alive.

At first glance it could be seen in what condition
the travellers were, so it was immediately necessary
to show joy at their arrival, to save the guests embarrassment.

"Those who have journeyed to the south have
come! Ak! the mighty, far-away travellers!" they
shouted, and helped the dogs pull the sled up the
slope.

The miserable dogs, starved to nothing, dull and
without strength! But now, when they came to people and heard other dogs howl and smelled the smell
of meat and old blubber, they suddenly decided to
forget their tiredness and be journey-glad again. They
kicked out their hind legs and pulled, wanting to
arrive at the settlement with the rush of bear dogs, to
frighten the children and fill the people with wonder.

There came no feast with the sleds, nor any gifts for friends who had been remembered. These were three men who had been remembered. These were one of them was a white man! So—there must be conditions under which even one of those is crushed down, and must take help from the people of this land, in spite of their wretchedness!

For this reason Mayark decided to show himself as magnificent as possible in his hospitality. Yes, his feast should become a legend! Therefore, so· many provisions were brought in that they hardly left room for the guests in the house. They had to lie on walrus meat and frozen bear hams. This day they walked on food in Mayark's house!

Among the guests was also Quitlak, known as the worst catcher of the tribe, but, at the same time, as the biggest eater. Mayark decided to make even him more than filled—that would be a triumph!

"Have meat cooked!" he shouted. "Ak! there is no worthy cooking here. Now there is shame in my house because of the incompetence of my wife!"

The people could barely laugh at his self-mockery, for by this time they were so full. And when Mayark saw that even Quitlak was beginning to chew slowly and with a thoughtful expression, he brought in little auks preserved in blubber.

' He continued to serve food. He had sun-dried auks, which he served with the excuse that they were so poorly supplied in his house that they had to permit this bird meat to play the role of food! Now his joy was so overpowering that he himself had to laugh with them. He had long been watching the astonishment of the others, had seen his generosity richly rewarded with overfilling and loud shouting, and so his joy was very strong.

"Bring something eatable in!" he roared, and fetched frozen seal liver and seal blubber which was fresh and light pink. They all felt that, in spite of their heavy stomachs, water could still run in their mouths, and it expected to be mixed with something new. They bit into the liver and it was as if one were given summer into one's mouth. The blood dripped over their fingers and their chins and cheeks were smeared with color, so that one thought of berries that had been crushed.

Yes, at Mayark's house the summer sprang into the people, and as always happens when one has eaten much blood-enriching nourishment, speech became gay and laughing loud.

While the others continued eating, Bozi slept for a little while. Then he was again like a young dog that knows neither fatigue nor trouble. Forgotten was the excitement of the journey, the endless trip behind the sled in the cold, with hunger and fear for travelling companions. He no longer thought of the iceberg which had fallen on them but had missed its revenge. Nor of that which had driven him back in a hurry and with care in his eyes. Ak! he had forgotten all about that. He thought of life and joy and the feast. He stood up, shouting and laughing, like the others.

There was more life. More laughter sounded and some of the guests kicked the food which lay piled high on the floor. And a few of them threw the rest of it into the house passage, where the young dogs, or whoever else wanted to, could eat it or let it spoil. On such a night nothing was taken back to the meat racks, as was usual. There was only life and dizziness in their heads, and strength in their bodies.

One of the guests jumped up and sang. Often he who sings first is embarrassed, and first prepares the others for his low ability to entertain them with song. But not on this night, at Mayark's! He who sang did not think of a counter-singer; no one needed to stand opposite him and help him with his song.

It was an elderly man who began, and he gave his song to everyone. It was only a little poem which was born of joy, and which put into words the memory of many seals in an ice fissure. And when he was through, another followed. And then another. The rest hummed and ate the bloody liver. Fire came into their bodies, and they thought of white men, who often were filled with too much joy to keep it closed up in their mouths. That happened to them because of bottles, but here one had frozen liver.

Now old Darm reached for the drum. Yes, it had even come to the time when women should sing with the men. Thus the joy became immeasurably great, and this night would be talked about all along the coast.

Darm stood with her feet spread wide. She had thrown off her under fur and her hair fluttered. She looked wild as she danced to the music she beat out of the drum. She swayed her upper body from side to side, her fat back shook, and her old, withered breasts flopped against her sides and gave her bellowing more rhythm than the drum itself. Her knot of hair fell from her head, and often her face was completely covered as it fell around her in thick rings. Her face, even to her mouth and eyes, was smeared with blood, and the sight and sound of her wildness brought the others to silence.

> The ones who travel to the South have returned
>   home—!
> The ones who travel to the South have returned
>   home—!
> Zatok, the newly married, has returned home,
> His wife already holds herself in readiness
> For the joy of the far travellers—!
> Ha ja, Ha ja ja, Ha ja ja, Ja!

Her song was a woman's idea of joy and the words of a woman about things which she knew. Let trappers sing of the doings of a bear, and women of the night!

Bozi's senses were aflame and his eyes fastened on Arnanguak. Did he perhaps understand the glance of a woman, when she herself did not? He jumped to the bed plank on which she was sitting with no underclothes except her underpants. He put his hand on her leg and touched her breasts, which were firm and smooth.

A woman's skin gives a man peace. Lightly he passed his hand up and down her body, but then he let his hand drop and she noticed he did not look at her. She saw that memories came to him from the touch of her, and he looked at no one, only stared in front of him, and his face forgot to smile. But a woman knows when her time has come, for every man feels, at some time, that women have to be considered as people.

Arnanguak was little and young yet, but she had been tried out by many men. Each time a stronger one had taken her, though so far not one had demanded her from her father for life. Now it seemed as though she wanted to be the one to demand. She did not want to feel Bozi's hand slip away, and she took it and with silent strength laid it again on her body. But Bozi resisted, for his thoughts were in a land where a woman had robbed him of joy.

Old Darm sat on the floor and sang. She had excited herself into a frenzy—her mouth foamed, her hair was stiff and standing up on her head. Her brown hands, with their long, crooked black nails, were trembling on the drum, and her voice became deep and hoarse like a man's, as she sang on. When saliva flowed from her mouth and splashed on one of the bystanders, he, too, was infected by her fire. All the men had joined in the singing. So, also, had the women, and their piping sounded high and shrill, as though they were of a different land from the men. Yes, it sounded as though they felt themselves to be high up, on top of a mountain, and unreachable.

Darm also sang about the white man, and those who were still laughing turned toward him and saw that Bozi had really let the life of the people become his own—they saw him with his hand on one of their women.

At this Mayark burst into a shout that was even louder than the bellowing of Darm. She stopped singing immediately, for she was a woman among men and had practically used up her strength. Mayark was calling for their attention and all understood. Darkness—darkness—there should be complete darkness in the house, to surround everybody. There were noises—an iceberg calved in the room, bears growled, dogs howled—all the noises in the world were borrowed to be used in the house of Mayark at Cape York! No one knew whether he was a human being or a burning fire. Nobody knew anything because of the food and blood which they had stuffed into themselves and which seemed to flood them with the warmth of summer. Nobody knew anything because of the wild songs and the beating of the drum, the smell of women and of the skins on the bed plank.

Bozi noticed that Arnanguak had pulled his arm further around her—but he knew nothing. The magic of the song of the drum had taken his thoughts away from a woman in any other country—but he knew that here was one. He felt her—she had a head, breasts and a body. She was a woman.

And the lamps were turned down. Only in the far distance sounded the song of Darm. No—perhaps she was silent now, and it might be only the echo that was still locked in his head and could not escape. Now he had returned from his long journey to the south and was with the people whom he wanted to make his own.

The putting out of the lamps—Arnanguak—everything else was forgotten. There were no people in the world, nothing living. There was only one thing—this fire, which was taking hold of everyone, and which had completely consumed him.

In the morning Uvdluriak got up and looked after the dogs. The poor animals were haggard. Pulled into the strange house passage, they were given thawed-out food, as much as they could eat, then they were glad to get out again and continue their sleep. After their long, hard journey they needed rest.

When Bozi awoke, the house was in order. He rubbed his eyes. His bones ached, his back was tired, and his shoulders hurt. Only now came the effects of his long hardships, when he had the leisure to feel them.

The women of the house had taken his things and dried them. His boots were fixed and fresh grass had been put under his stockings. He put on his clothes and went out for a long walk, so that the air should take his heaviness from him. He met Torngé, who said that, unfortunately, the meat feast had not lasted long enough. "One must eat much to be free from worry—and a stomach is really much too small for the desires of man!"

Then Bozi saw Arnanguak.

"Arnanguak!" he called, and went to her. He took her hand but she pulled it back quickly. "Come," he said. "Let me talk to you."

"Just listen, and experience an impudence!" she said, looking at him. "A man wishes my coming in the middle of the day, and out in the open! Ak! I am spoken to by a man. Oho, hey!"

She ran inside quickly and Bozi stood there alone. He went up on a hill, climbing far up the slope. He who thinks strongly creates warmth in himself and does not freeze, and he thought of Arnanguak and of last night. And he thought even more of the woman in the faraway land, who had cheated him of his hopes. Without any happiness he thought of his future life.

It was not until evening that most of the people were again on their feet and going visiting from house to house. In this settlement one was given to eat so that one felt it.

Bozi also walked around, eating, and still found room in his intenstines for more. He went into the house occupied by the young people, and now they, too, wanted to show off. Two young men each brought a bundle of dried birds, as guest food. These were dipped into rancid walrus oil, which was several years old and which burned one's gullet. They were all full from eating yesterday and today, so several of them laid on the bed planks when the chewing tired them. Bozi was again lying next to Arnanguak and again his thoughts of white women disappeared. When he awoke, the lamps were turned out and he found the girl awake and completely conscious.

The night passed in darkness.

When he awoke again, there was still darkness around him. His fire had died out, and he felt as if he had climbed a steep mountain, over many obstacles in his way. He lay there for a while until he got accustomed to the grey light in the house, and saw the people sleeping around him.

Next to him lay Arnanguak. But she was without charm, and he was shocked that he had felt a desire for her caresses. He looked at her hair, unkempt and matted, and she was breathing like a seal in its breathing hole, and even in her sleep she was scratching herself, from lice. Then he looked at her dirty legs and other memories came to him, and he suddenly sat up. She awoke and put her arm on his shoulder, but he felt as though he had been hit with cold water. He shook off her hand and jumped to the floor. She thought, "He wishes to go on a catch, and bring me presents. I will be proud and happy." So she only turned over on the other side, boring into sleep, and pulled over herself the cover of the one lying next to her. But Bozi lay on the floor, next to another man, and he felt his anger mounting. This anger was not directed at others, only at himself.

It was he who woke the settlement on this morning. He wanted to get home quickly and, when he found out that the dogs were still too tired to go on, he decided to take others. Torngé and Uvdluriak could follow later. All the people said that their dogs were his, and three of them were ready to start with him immediately. They expected big events in Bozi's settlement, to celebrate his return.

As they went back and forth, preparing for the journey, Arnanguak came out of the house. Bozi stopped for a moment and looked at her—then shook his head and turned away.

Then it happened that she, herself, spoke to him. "Are you coming back again?"

Ak! Arnanguak got no answer. She became the talk of all the settlements. Arnanguak—have you heard of her?—the one who spoke to a man without first being spoken to by him!

Chapter Seventeen

THAT night Bozi and his companions reached a cave at Agpat, and here they decided to sleep. But one of his fellow travelers said that he had meat stored some distance further on, and that he would go on ahead and spend the night at that place. It was Quitlak, the big eater, who said this. The others laughed and said they did not remember his having mentioned anything about his big catch. But Quitlak paid no attention to their talk. He cracked his whip over his dogs and was gone.

He rode with a light load. Sittting on his sled, he let the ice run backwards under him. His dogs were in no hurry and he, himself, buried his thoughts so that the night should pass quickly.

Now and then he thought of how he would be received at Bozi's settlement. He decided to play the part of a man who was traveling through, journeying to the lee side, but had stopped on his way to visit them. Then, after he had been there for awhile, he could say something about the dangerous iceberg and he could tell them about Bozi, about the great feast, and the dogs they had lost. Quitlak was ready to give up the sleep of many nights to be the one to tell about these unusual events.

Much had happened in the settlement at Umanak while Bozi was away. The great Minik had returned. He had moved into Uvdluriak's house, wanting to take the place of the departed master. He did not speak to Ivalu right away, but when the night began he expressed shameless thoughts. Ivalu ran out and did not come back again that night.

But something even worse happened. Minik went to Elias, who had been left in charge of Bozi's possessions and who was supposed to live in his big house with the deaf and dumb boy.

"It has proven itself unsatisfactory that Bozi should trade with the people of this land," Minik said to Elias. "I intend to journey to the white men, in the summer, with a ship. Then I shall return with great possessions and give away goods without pay."

Elias said nothing. He was still a stranger in this land and could not banish his fear of the people. Now he knew no way out, but he quietly told Minik that Bozi had said he was not to be allowed in the house. At this Minik began to be terrible. His voice became very loud and his words were like a foaming river. He got up and grabbed a harpoon shaft on which Elias was putting a new point. He swung it so wildly that Elias had to jump to one side. Uzugodark, the deaf and dumb boy, remained quietly seated. It was amusing to him to watch Minik's mouth when his talk came fast, and finally he, too, went and stood

276

next to Minik, and began to make violent sounds at Elias.

Suddenly Elias began to cry: "Ak! Now there is no more doubt. I always had a queer feeling about having to be with a man who was marked by the Lord! Surely Uzugodark has now called down curses on me with his incomprehensible sounds, just because for a few days I neglected to give him bread, although I ate. Now I am going to flee from this house which holds only enemies!"

He ran out and up to the houses of the people. Ak! How great was his homesickness! He thought that now he would surely die, for no one could endure more than he had endured, and live.

Those who listened felt sorry for him. Samik said that Elias would surely have more pleasure if he moved into his house.

Elias became quieter. He said that although others had advised him to flee, this would mean death, and at Samik's would be his only chance of remaining alive.

From Bozi's provisions Minik took whatever he could use. Later they found he had taken two guns, many cartridges, and clothing. The people were going to visit him, but when they saw that he had prepared the food Bozi had brought from his own land, they would not join him in the meal. At this Minik laughed very much, saying that it was Bozi who should ask permission to stay in this country as he was a stranger, and not born here like Minik or the others.

The next day he took a hammer and forced open the large boxes which were standing in Bozi's room, and took whatever he wished. He was so pleased with this that he took another gun and gave it to Uzugo-dark. He began to drink from the bottles which he found. Then he ran into the houses, calling to the people and saying that he wished to have guests— that he was going to serve everyone good things to eat and no one would leave without presents. Some of the people went, but others feared the conse-quences. Merquzaq said that the man appeared as a thief in their settlement and one must, therefore, feel ashamed and show him contempt.

A few of the women went to Minik. But although they evidently did not seem worth winning, still he gave them needles, thread and scissors before sending them away.

Women should often be kept away from the talk of men. But that is impossible, as there is no language understood by men alone, and some of the women heard the men talking of how Minik had refused those who had gone to show him love. The men laughed about it—but men whose deeds evoke laugh-ter awaken curiosity in women. And Ivalu began to think.

Ak! For so long now her life had found no changes. She happened to be one of those who did not wish all her days to be alike. Minik was a man who caused talk. He had had many experiences and now he created experiences for others. So she decided to go to him. She thought: "Anyway, when he begins to talk to me about his desire, I shall have nothing good to answer him, and that will be amusing. My grandmother is dead and all I do is sit at home and chew skins for my grandfather. Yes, it will be very amusing!"

She knew she was not without power. She saw the men turn their heads toward her when she got undressed in the evening. She had often seen hands reach out for her when visitors slept in the house—the hands of men who had their own wives lying next to them. At such times she would call out loudly: "Keep away from me! Stay where you are, next to your wife, and leave me alone! You are a shameless guest; you are married to a woman and you have made no agreement with anybody else for her, have you?"

So now she wanted to go to Minik. She would let him feel her, and let his hand slip over her. But then she was going to run home and the other women would not understand why she was running away from such a powerful man, one who could invite people to eat of the white man's food and to drink strong drink from the bottles. Ak! It would be very amusing!

When she entered his house, Minik did not have a clear look. His eyes were clouded, his walk was dizzy, and the visitors felt peculiar. Uzugodark had been permitted to drink from the bottles and he was running around like a little dog that could not walk straight.

"Herewith one comes to visit," Ivalu said, and remained standing at the door, looking around for awhile.

Minik said his house was not easy to fill, because few of the people would visit him. He went back and forth in the rooms and was terrible to look at. His face was smeared with the red paint of the sweet berries which he ate with sugar. Suddenly he stood by the door and said that as the people did not wish to eat the food he was offering, he had no desire to have them as guests and therefore he would like it better if they all went home.

His words made them all leave, but Ivalu had just come and she did not think she should go with the first ones to depart. She noticed that besides herself there was only one little boy left in the place. She started for the door, but Minik grabbed her with both hands and held her tight, shouting to the little boy to get out. The others stood outside and began to laugh. They tried to look into the house through the windows, but the window plates were frozen.

Minik forced her to drink from the bottles—and no one saw either of them for the next few days. Then she came out, but with Minik following her closely it was not possible for her to run away. So she showed herself indifferent; no one should see that she was unhappy and bemoaning what had happened.

People noticed that smoke was coming from the top of the house. Food is being prepared, they thought. Some of the women talked about going in to visit, as there must be news which would be amusing to hear. But they did not have time, for out of the darkness came Quitlak, with very tired dogs and no load on his sled.

They saw immediately that he must be a man who had left his home settlement in a great hurry and had important news to communicate. They rushed to him, but he jumped from his sled, swung his whip, and shouted that his dogs were dangerous and should be feared for their ferocity. But it did no good. The people only laughed. Quitlak was well known, and they knew his dogs liked being touched by strangers, as they were so seldom given food by their master.

As his arrival caused only much laughter, Quitlak decided to tell his story immediately.

"Those who journeyed to the south almost never returned," he called, without any greeting.

His words made them all stand still—but Quitlak decided to say no more until he had eaten, and was lying undressed on a bed plank. A man who is ready to crawl into sleep tells his story with calmness and delight, and that was what Quitlak decided to do.

But now Kazaluk, Uvdluriak's wife, and Torngé's wife came running. They did not wish to question him directly about their husbands, so they stood there until Quitlak had said a little more. Now he had the whole settlement listening to him, and each time he gave them a little more of what he knew his words traveled from one mouth to another. Later, when he sat in a house, he was a mighty man. His story was now known, but he had not told them all the details of the things that had happened.

Quitlak ate well, and his dogs had full bellies and were already asleep. Only then did the people remember that they, too, had great things to report: about Minik, who had taken all of Bozi's property, and about Ivalu, who was with him. And old Merquzaq was sorry that Bozi was weak and without great power, as there was no great battle with Minik to look forward to.

Now everybody thought of Minik. Some of them got the desire to visit him and ask how he would meet the new event of Bozi's return. But when they got

to the house, something happened. Ivalu came running through the door. After her ran Minik. They
saw him grab her by the shoulders from behind, then
take her around the waist and lift her off the ground
so that her legs and arms waved in the air like four
kayak paddles. She screamed aloud and he ran back
into the house, carrying her. Then he locked the door,
and now they were married, for he was beating her.
But it had happened without her family's consent.

They heard Minik shouting loud with anger and
once they heard Ivalu scream with pain. The men
thought of their own women, with whom they could
also not live in peace until they had once beaten them
into submission.

"Such is the nature of mankind," Samik said. The
people went home and told what they had seen.

In the evening Quitlak went to many houses. He
was full of stories and the people made him far from
empty of food. As some of them entered a house
where Quitlak had been invited to eat walrus meat,
they heard the screams of a woman coming from
Bozi's house.

"Again Ivalu wants to differ with her new husband," they said. Then they laughed a little and
went in to listen to the man with many tales.

The night grew old before everybody was asleep.
Only one could not stop thinking, and that was old
Merquzaq. He lay there for awhile, and then got

up, went out, and harnessed his dogs. Bozi was on his way home, and from Quitlak's words it was clear that Bozi knew nothing about Minik. Therefore he thought it best to warn him. Merquzaq thought it would not be right if Bozi were to come home and Minik were to stand in the door and shoot. Who felt more strongly than he about asking help for his grandchild? His old wife, Ama, had died during Bozi's absence. Ak! Merquzaq's mind was filled with many worries!

Therefore he rode, now, to meet Bozi, and nobody paid any attention to the direction in which he drove.

It was almost light when Merquzaq came upon Bozi and his sled companions. He was bringing warning and information, so he had no reason to make it lengthy or thrilling. While they listened to Merquzaq's story about Minik, both of Bozi's companions looked at him. He, like all white men, became completely silent, and made his mouth small and closed it tight.

"Keep on speaking. Why did Elias run away?"

"His fear became greater than his strength. But I am certain that the people of the settlement will help you, for it is not good to have one's own countryman as master."

Bozi said they were to drive fast. Merquzaq took

him on his sled, and at this the men from Cape York were displeased.

"Is it believed that our dogs cannot run as fast as the dogs from the middle fjords?"

They tied new lashes on their whips. Bozi and Merquzaq heard the other dogs whine continuously as they rushed on ahead.

"Let the others get to Umanak ahead of us," Merquzaq said. "If Minik is dangerous and wishes to kill, then it is good that many who can stop him should surround him!"

From then on the old man sat still. He spoke no more, only watched the dogs. They were the dogs of an old man and therefore had not much practice in fast running. Bozi asked him if he were not afraid that the help and warning he had brought would bring anger upon him ,too.

"If I had room for fear in my body," Merquzaq said, "I would have been without life for many suns. I am old, and no great damage can grow out of my fate, even if I die. My little grandchild is the only thing that is in my thoughts, even though she is already grown up and does not ask my advice any more. Only when she is older, and I am sleeping on the hill, will she think of me."

Bozi's thoughts, also, now pursued Ivalu. It was a long time since he had thought of her. Her face was different from the others' and her talk was more

sensible. But he had decided that no other woman
should ever be in his life again. That letter had made
him feel like this, and his meeting with Arnanguak.
All women reminded him of the one in his own land.
That was why he had not thought of Ivalu's face, or
her supple body. He only wanted to create peace in
his house and order among the people. So he, too, sat
silent for a long time. The snow sprayed backwards
under the sled and Merquzaq whipped the dogs, who
fell into a gallop so as not to be too far behind the
others.

As they approached the house they saw a large
group of people standing in front of it. The sled
stopped in the midst of a great many people who were
calling and shouting in disorder, so that it was difficult to understand their words. They were calling a
welcome to Bozi, and shouting that again there was
a white man in their settlement, which made it different from any other.

Before either of them could get off the sled Elias
was pulling off his mitten and offering his hand in
greeting.

"Ak! We are glad to see you! Here in this place
great danger ruled, but there is great good fortune
to report now. The joy is great, for Minik has gone!"

Then he told Bozi that Minik had left during the
night.

"Is this your joy, Elias?" Bozi asked, with a little

anger. "It is not good for the ears to hear that many things under your care were taken away and used up!"

"Ak! I am a bad guardian of other people's possessions," Elias said. "I am of no use, any more, and this time I have been specially unfit!"

He moaned continuously, until Bozi was forced to comfort him and say that many things showed he was not to blame. But Elias said he could not see how anyone could be more miserable than he. "It would be best if I were dead," he said, "but unfortunately I am still alive to anger you."

Bozi entered the house and saw immediately that Minik had taken with him many clothes and instruments, and the largest part of his whiskey. A few guns were also missing. Uzugodark had one. He held it in his hand and laughed. He seemed to want to show Bozi his pride in his new gun, and that he was a catcher like the others.

Elias asked if he was to make a fire and prepare food. He said he knew he should have done it sooner, but his fear kept him from going into the house until Bozi entered. Bozi told him to prepare food but to be quick about it, as they had to journey again immediately.

"To journey?" Elias asked. "But you have just come. You need have no fear, and you need not flee already today. Minik has left for the north, and many sleeps will pass before he returns. He has taken a wife with him who will make his life beautiful!"

Bozi laughed at this, and they all saw that Elias had been stupid. So they all laughed at him, but their laughter became a little quieter when Bozi said he was going after Minik, take away the things he had stolen, and tell him things that would put fear on his sled, to remain there forever.

Bozi asked how many dogs Minik had and if they were fast. He ordered Elias, whose dogs had been lying still for a long time, and another man whose team was also rested, to go with him. The other man was Samik. He began to prepare for the journey immediately, and told the young men to bring some dog meat out of his shed.

In a short while they were ready to start.

It was evening by now, but the moon shone and they had only to follow the tracks left by Minik's sled, which were easy to see. Bozi sat on Elias' sled and Elias drove. A long time passed before they had to stop and untangle the harness. Bozi was so full of thoughts of getting on that he walked ahead. The two others talked, and told each other it surely was not the best thing to be the first to reach Minik! There was the possibility that he would shoot. . . .

It took them a long time to catch up with Bozi. They drove very slowly, so that the white man finally had to stop and wait for them. At this they were very glad, for they thought that now he had decided either to return or at least make camp for the night.

"The dogs are tired and cannot go on," Elias said. "It seems best to make camp."

But Bozi took the whip himself and drove on, and the dogs fell into a good pace. Then Elias began to moan, complaining about his fate, saying he was never destined to fight and now he was to be killed against his will. For surely Minik would kill them all.

Bozi told him he was a coward and that he should not act like a sick man. That gave Elias the idea that he really was sick. He began to cry, and said he had a big pain all over his body, and that he had not been feeling well even before they had left.

Bozi held his dogs back to wait for Samik. When the big man caught up with Bozi he said that his little daughter had just come into his mind, and that it would be wrong if he did not return. He told Bozi that when thoughts of one who is far away come to a traveller, it means that something will happen to the one whom these thoughts concern.

"Well, if you wish to leave me now, then let it be so," Bozi said. "No one need help me who does not want to. Journey home and tell them of your great deeds, for your tongue seems to be the strongest thing about you!"

Then Elias began to cry loudly. Was he, then, to

remain alone with a white man who was strange in his land, and be felled by a mad enemy with a gun? "And besides," he wailed, "I am sick myself, without any strength. And our dogs are bad. Ak! Yes, yes, I am seriously unhappy and am to be pitied!"

Bozi stopped for awhile and then made a decision.

"You both shall return, and neither of you shall accompany me to Minik. But I am a white man and I want my things. I forbade Minik to come back, and he did it anyway. For this I want to see him, and also to take Ivalu away from him, as she was taken against her will. But you are to return and tell the catchers to follow me after they have rested. They should follow my tracks until they find me."

The two others said that that was by far the best thing to do, and that they saw Bozi was a man who knew how to forge plans which would turn out luckily.

"Many will follow to help you. We can be more useful by securing sleds to follow you. That will show that you are a master here in this land."

Bozi took all the furs and provisions which were on the sleds. Then they turned Samik's sled around and whipped the dogs homeward. Bozi looked after them until they disappeared.

It did not seem to him that the dogs showed tiredness, nor the men illness, as they ran for home.

Chapter Eighteen

BOZI'S dogs were a little disappointed that they could not go south with the others. He had to keep after them continually—he could never put down his whip. Therefore his thoughts were occupied and weariness left him. Just to keep going and catch Minik—that was all he wanted.

The tracks showed that Minik had taken the road to the big foothills, and there, Bozi thought, he would have camped. There was hope of finding him. . . .

He was right. Minik was there.

But the Minik he found was not a Minik with fighting in his mind. He was lying in a cave, and Bozi saw immediately that he was drunk. As he saw his enemy approaching, Minik shouted threats. But he was so drunk it would have been impossible for him to carry them out.

He lay half inside, with his sled and guns standing in front of the cave entrance. Bozi took the guns and then interrupted Minik's bellowing.

"Minik!" he said. "You knew you were forbidden to come back to Umanak, but you came anyway. You stole some of my possessions and you drove Elias from my house. You carried off Ivalu against her will. Therefore I am very angry—and I am going to punish you!"

"Ak! Yes," Minik answered. "I understand. It is Ivalu you want—whom I have taken as a wife for myself. Yes! Yes! You are stealing my wife. I warn you—this shall not remain untold in your land!"

Ivalu was sitting on some skins, and would not get up. Bozi ordered her to leave Minik, but she did not answer. From this Bozi thought that now she was satisfied with her husband, and felt sorry for him.

"So—you are one who would stand by a thief!" he said angrily. "You want to be the wife of a man whose words one cannot believe, who breaks into other people's houses and does things which are shameful! Ak! Ivalu, now I see your thoughts are different from what I had believed. Now I know that all over the world women are alike—they get pleasure from lies and wrong thoughts!"

Ivalu found no words for her defense and her fear of the angry man was increasing. As he kept speaking she grew more and more afraid, for he seemed to be getting excited at his own words, and forgetting that it was Minik who had made him so angry.

She felt like a child. Words which would relieve her fear would not come to her, and she began to cry. She did not cry aloud, but the violence of her sobs shook her whole body.

Minik saw this, and tried to turn Bozi's thoughts in a different direction. He put out his arm for Ivalu, trying to appear as a great man protecting his wife.

But when he touched her she only cried harder and pushed him away. Bozi grabbed him and forced him up on his feet—but Minik was too full of drunkenness to stand. He fell down, and tried in vain to get up again. Bozi dragged him out of the cave.

The dogs were still harnessed to Minik's sled— one could see he had been thinking only of his bottle. Ivalu must have had to take in the skins on which she slept. Everything was in disorder. The whip was lying among the dogs, who had taken the meat off the sled and eaten most of it. If it had not been for this, they would not have even been fed.

Bozi stood over the drunken man.

"Get out—and as fast as you can!" he ordered. "Go farther away than anyone has ever been, and remember that from now on you are never to enter my house again. Not until you come with a different mind, and have done things which will make people admire you."

Minik became a little more assured. He had expected death for what he had done. But now he saw that his punishment was not very great, so he talked again:

"Let me take my wife with me. Without her I can have no clothes made nor my catch prepared."

"Yes," Bozi said. "Take your woman with you, and both of you stay out of my sight! But everything you have stolen from me must be paid for. Each year you must send me a sled full of fox-skins until you are told that you have sent enough."

But these words filled Ivalu with terror.

"You must not give me to Minik! I am frightened of this man, and if I oppose him it will mean death for me. No one must give me to him! Look—see why I cannot go. See why I remained seated when you came in! He has torn off my clothes, and if I had run away, I would have frozen. But now that I have seen you I know that freezing would be better than being his wife. For what is Minik, compared to you and your greatness?"

Ivalu had said too much and later she was ashamed of these words. But now she was angry and afraid, and did not think of a woman's modesty.

"Ak!" Bozi roared. "So he has harmed you? He has used force against you? Then he shall feel my anger!"

He threw himself on Minik and began to beat him, and like a dog Minik had to take the beating. He yelled with pain as Bozi's fists poured blows on his body. His face became bruised and bloody, but Bozi continued without stopping. Whenever Minik fell, Bozi pulled him to his feet and hit him again and again, sometimes with his clenched fists and sometimes with the palm of his hand. Minik's blood splashed like water when his face was hit, but he could not run away because Bozi was quick and blocked his way. He couldn't fall down and lie there, either, for when he tried Bozi brought him to his feet with kicks and more beatings.

To listen to his yelling and moaning was a pleasure for Ivalu. Women like strong men, and their admiration falls on the one who is the stronger. Because of what Minik had done to her she could feel no pity for him.

Bozi continued the beating until it seemed as though he were a man without thoughts. He kept on hitting him, and if Minik covered any part of himself with his hands and arms, Bozi hit him where he was not covered. He smashed his ears, bruised his shoulders and thighs, beat his nose flat, and cut a wound over each eye so that the blood gushed down his face. He finally hit Minik one terrible blow on the chin, and he fell and lay there.

Ivalu sat there trembling. No one bothered about her, and although she was frightened, still she was pleased. Now she was a woman for whom men were fighting, and she forgot that Bozi had directed his anger against her, too. She was shaking with excitement. Here she sat in a mountain cave, watching a fight, and unable to run away even if she had wanted to, because her clothes had been torn off her and her boots were lying in a corner, cut to pieces.

Bozi stopped, and looked down at the man on the ground. Then he kicked him and went over to the sleds. Ivalu heard him fumbling with the dogs. First he harnessed his own, then he straightened out Minik's ropes and got his sled ready. He took skins and provisions from his own sled and tied them on Minik's. After he had finished he came back to Minik, who was lying on the ground and was frightful to look at.

"Get up—you must travel!" he said, but Minik hardly moved. He was not completely without thoughts, for when Bozi leaned down and grabbed his shoulder he lifted his arms to protect himself from more blows.

"No more sleeping," Bozi said. "And if you ever come near me again before you have paid what you owe me, you will be punished like today, only more severely! Get up and go to your sled. It is straightened out, and I have put a new lash on your whip. Your dogs ate the other while you were drinking from my bottles. Go now—and drive fast and far. And—your way is not in the direction in which I go!"

He dragged him to the sled, and Minik woke up and began to moan. Bozi paid no attention to him. He came back to get Minik's coat, with which Ivalu had covered herself, as if to hide under it. But Bozi took it from her, leaving her to cover herself with other skins.

"Hock! Hock!" she heard Bozi call. He put Minik's sled on its way, and she could tell from the howling of the dogs that it was going further and further away. When Bozi returned he said that now they were alone.

Two of them alone in a cave—and she had no clothes! This was a difficult thing for a woman, when the other was a white man, so Ivalu was silent. A long time passed before either of them spoke. She looked down at the skins which she had pulled over her legs. It seemed to her that only now was misfortune overtaking her. For, since the death of her husband, she had only had happiness when she was visiting Bozi— and now he was standing before her and seeing her in a miserable condition. She had clothes only for her upper body, and where was she going to get clothes for the rest?

After awhile she raised her head slowly and looked at Bozi's feet, standing right in front of her. They did not move. She sat that way for a long time, and then she had the thought that it was wrong of him not to say something, and a light anger grew in her. It gave her the strength to look up, and she saw that he was looking at her. Their eyes met.

"Little Ivalu," he said, "I would be happy if you were pleased that Minik cannot annoy you any more."

"It is not impossible that that is the case. Perhaps I am a little glad over it."

"Only a little?"

White men never understand modest speech, and always demand shameless answers. She did not say anything, but there was gratefulness in her look.

"It will be necessary to get you clothes for your trip home," he said. "Have you needles to sew with? I have a few things in my sack that you can put on until you make yourself others. Maybe your pants can be fixed, and you can sew your boots enough to serve for a little while. Then we can leave for home—and when we arrive there you can have new skins."

Bozi now started to straighten out things. He brought his possessions in, and built a fire close to the entrance of the cave. In a box he had the thing which she had heard him call a primus stove, and he lighted it.

For a while Ivalu sat and watched him. She couldn't help him, for without clothes one is of little use. Bozi handed her the pieces of her pants, and she quickly stuffed them under the cover, filled with shame because he saw her do it and knew she was nearly undressed. Then they ate together, and drank tea, but they did not talk much because Ivalu said very little when he asked questions. She felt that what Minik had done should be quickly forgotten, and not talked about.

After they had finished eating Bozi told her how Elias and Samik had accompanied him, but had gotten sick with fright and so he had to come on alone. Ivalu laughed and said it was good the others could not see her here, like this, for they were incapable of creating thoughts for themselves, and so their tongues ran away very easily and they would tell everything they saw. Then a little more time passed in which neither of them said anything, and Bozi began to notice that the cold was crawling up his legs. He was sorry he had given Minik so many skins, for now he did not have enough to make a bed for each of them. He told Ivalu that he was very tired, as he had not slept for a long time.

"We must sleep close to one another," he said. "For there are not enough covers for two."

Ivalu said no, she wanted to sleep alone. But she said it in a low voice, for she realized she had no choice. When he pulled off his boots and lay down beside her, her resistance was not great. They had to sleep close together, for the cover was narrow. Finally Bozi decided to bring in the sled and make up their bed close to it. That way they could keep warmer, and the cover would not slip off during the night. While he was doing this she helped him, and they talked. This made them both feel easier. It was difficult, and they laughed over it—and this laughing decided their whole future life.

Bozi was already more than a husband when he again took off his boots. He stood for a second on the hide, letting his bearskin pants slide down his bare legs. When he lay down he pulled the fur over his head, and he had to put his arm around her shoulders in order to get under the same cover with her. One never talks so quietly and without deception as one does when sleeping close to someone.

"We must not be ashamed, for we must lie this way if we want to save our lives," Bozi said. Ivalu understood that what he said was right. But still she said nothing; she thought only of the words he had first spoken when he came into the cave and saw her lying next to Minik.

She began to cry again and Bozi did not stop her, but after a little time her sobs stopped by themselves. They lay there quietly and were just with one another. They both felt the cold and Bozi asked her if she were freezing. She put his hand on her legs and then he noticed that they were uncovered, and cold as rocks in the winter.

"Take care of your legs," he said, pulling her close to him. "Why do you lie there without covering yourself?"

"It happens that one is a little embarrassed," she said.

"Ivalu," Bozi said, "sad things have happened to you. I do not know how you feel about them but I, too, am unhappy. A woman of my own land has proven herself full of lies to me. That was told me by a letter, while I was in the south. Therefore my mind, too, is dark and I have heavy thoughts."

They were both shivering with cold. Only after they had pressed their bodies close to each other, without thinking about it, did they feel their warmth go from one to the other. They lay quietly for a little while, until Bozi said: "It is dark, and we cannot see one another's faces. Let us make a light, and then we can get up and pull the sled even closer to the side of the cave. That will make our bed very narrow, and we will be close to one another and warm one another, so that the night will pass in sleep and we will be strengthened for tomorrow's journey home."

They got up and did as he said, neither looking at the other, so that neither should be embarrassed. When they lay down, close together, as was now necessary, Bozi said they should have done this in the first place and then they would not have frozen.

After a little while Ivalu said that she was thinking of her clothes which would have to be sewn. Her fingers would need the help of her eyes, and it would not be light until it was time for them to leave. Bozi told her that by that time he would find a way and he promised that everything would be arranged. Men always make promises like that, but Ivalu knew it was impossible for him to help her. She knew she would have to do the sewing herself, so she laughed at him a little. He laid his hand on her face, saying he wanted to feel the lines of it because it was so nice to look at, and he said her eyes were like a light in a house, shining out over the ice in the darkness.

"Talk more like this," Ivalu said. "Now words are spoken which I love to hear."

"Ivalu," Bozi said, "I have always thought that you were different from the other women here on this coast."

Then she told him how, when she played as a child, she would dream that a white man was taking her. She told him how she had thought that Peary was her father, and how surprised she was when he had sent her away with the sled. "Later I got used to the people again, but I could never forget the white men."

Bozi was lying still. He loosened his grip on her body.

"Ivalu," he said, "Ivalu, I have told you that I never want to have a woman again. I believe that the truth is not great in the bosoms of women."

"Yes," she said, "you said that. But I am truthful, and I never use a lie in my talk."

Again they were quiet. Then he said it was strange how things happened which had brought them so close together. "If someone were to come into this cave he would think we were married, and not just strangers who had been brought together by accident."

"Yes," said Ivalu, "it is strange, but I feel it is good."

"Why do you say that?"

"Because I say what I am thinking. I have told you—I do not use lies in my speech."

Again he said nothing, and all the movements of his hands stopped. As she began to fear that his anger was rising again he suddenly grabbed her tightly around the neck and pressed his face against hers. He put his mouth over her mouth. Even in love the ways of the white men were different from the ways of the people, but to her it seemed as if it were summer, and as though she were closing her eyes and the sun was shining on her face. She wanted Bozi to do everything he wanted to do with her. Everything Minik had done reminded her of bad smells, but Bozi . . . Bozi . . . She had no will of her own any more, but there was great strength in her arms. She folded them around his neck, and learned how to put her mouth to his.

Later, Bozi awoke with a start. He raised his head, and in the same moment Ivalu, too, was without sleep.

"Did you hear a noise?"

"Yes—it is the wind that is growing. It is blowing hard in front of the cave, and coming from the southwest. It can become very strong here in the foothills."

Ivalu told him that she had been here with her

grandfather. The weather had held them for many days, and finally they had to go over the mountain to Netzilik to save themselves, for the ice broke up.

"I will go and look after the dogs. They are lying on the ice, and if it breaks up and drifts away, we may lose them."

"Dogs should always be tied on land, at the edge of the ice, in such a place as this. On the thin ice, with the new snow on it, it is much colder for them."

Bozi had to admit she was right—but a man does not wish to be taught by a woman, so he did not answer her.

"Can you find my things?" he asked her.

She found them. "A man should put his clothes under his sleeping skin," she said. "Then they are always found quickly, and are warm and pleasant when one puts them on."

Again she was right, but still he did not answer her. When he went outside the storm had begun. The dogs got up as though they had been expecting him, and were willing to come up on the solid ground. They pulled him up with them, then he ran back to her.

"Where is my knife? I must have my knife to make a hole, and then I can tie the dogs. It is snowing and the weather is bad. If only the ice doesn't break up—"

Ivalu sat up and said it was better to leave the dogs

free. "In a snowstorm they do not run away—and they can protect themselves better when they are not tied. Just leave them in their harness."

"Ak! I am a miserable white man who knows nothing himself," he said, and let the dogs stay free. Soon he was again at her side, but already he had difficulty in beating the snow out of his clothes. They lay there and listened to the storm.

"Perhaps you are a little angry that I spoke to you and gave you advice," Ivalu said to him. "But I only said what I did because I feel sorry for you. I have heard many of the people laugh at you when you have gone out for catch with them. You do not know the ways of the people which make things easy."

Bozi said he was glad to have her tell him this. "But after you have lived with me and have helped me, then I will have learned everything and you will not hear them laugh at my behavior any more."

"Ak! If you want me to live with you, then you must never say any words which are not your own," Ivalu said. "You must never speak words which are full of lies."

Outside the storm raged, but inside the cave were two people who were very close to each other, for they were not separated by any lies.

What they had feared would happen, happened. When Bozi went out in the morning the ice was gone. The sea lay black before them, and where he had first tied the dogs there were now waves. He went back and told her what he had seen. She looked at him with a question in her eyes.

"Will the sewing take long?" he asked. "Don't you think it would be better if you put on my clothes? Just so you can keep warm on the way?"

He went out again and looked at the moving water. It gave him a peaceful feeling to see something besides ice. In him many new thoughts were born. He didn't want to think of hatred any more. He wanted to close out the land of the white man, and be a man to enjoy life here with Ivalu, who was to become his wife and never leave him. And she would help him to have an easy mind.

Ivalu sewed until her fingers became stiff with cold. Then she would put them under the covers or on her body for a while, until they became warm. Then she would start again. Small pieces of the fox skins which Minik had torn to pieces in his madness were patiently put together, and some parts were patched with pieces of the reindeer-skin cover. By evening a pair of pants was ready.

Bozi went out to find the road, and when he returned the cave seemed like a home to him. It was afternoon, and dark, and Bozi made a light and then lighted the primus stove. They ate and drank and then lay down on the bed.

"There is not enough to fix my boots with," Ivalu said. "The dogs chewed up almost everything before you arrived."

He said she could put on his spare boots. They were too big, but she said that until they got to a place where there were people she would put skins inside them to fill them out.

"We are going home to our own house," Bozi said, "not to the house of other people."

"Is it really true that I am to live with you in your big house?"

"Yes, of course you shall live with me. Are we not man and wife? Have we not decided to remain always together? You must understand that what is mine shall also be yours. Our possessions belong to us both equally."

"That is a little difficult for me to understand— and my head will not be able to stand thinking of all this."

Then she was quiet. Her face seemed peaceful, but her eyes squinted slightly, because thoughts were going so fast in her head. She felt as though her head would split, for soon there would be no room for so many thoughts. Then suddenly she smiled, and put her arms around his neck. It was not possible to sleep, for neither of them was calm inside. But they did not speak for a long time.

"We heard that you have a name in your land

which is different from Bozi," she said finally. "How does it sound?"

"Carl Boezen," he said. "See if you can say it."

"Kale Boze—Kar Bozene—Kal . . ." she interrupted herself and laughed. "My tongue is unwilling to speak bad words," she said.

He started to teach her. He spoke the name slowly, and she repeated it after him. "Karel Boezeen—Karel Boezeen—Karel Boezeen—Ak! Now I can say it! I will be the wife of a white man. I shall be a white woman myself, just as I have always wished to be. So it shows itself that desire can come true!"

The night came, and he thought of his country, with its closed houses and lights and soft beds. Now he was lying here and everything was different, but he was glad, and wished to be nowhere in the world except in this cave in the great foothills.

The next morning when they awoke they laughed very much. At first Ivalu did not want to put on Bozi's boots.

"I shall be full of shame when they see me and laugh at me—but it seems necessary that I should wear them, anyway."

She stuffed pieces of skin into the boots, put them on and tied them tightly. They reached up to her knees, but the short pants left a large part of her legs free, and she would freeze. But Ivalu said it did not matter. "When I was little I was used to old boot shafts, and they always slid down and left my legs bare like this, in the winter. Now I shall pretend I am little again, until I sew myself new boots with long stiff shafts."

But when they went out into the open the wind was very cold, and she froze. Then they decided to change, and she put on his pants. But they were so big that she could not walk in them. Again they laughed, but Ivalu said, "Now, surely, you will quickly tire of me. For I do not think that in your land women would spend so much time on clothes which, in the end, they cannot use." But Bozi told her that that happened very often in his country.

"Many will laugh," Ivalu said, "when they hear my story. When I left, I was forced to go away—but my going back is much different." She held her hand to his face, smiled, and was happy.

"Ivalu," he said, "we must never speak of Minik again. The storm may have killed him by now. We must never remember that which he did to you. I do not wish to hear his name again."

It was clear that a journey homeward was impossible. The water lay open and free in front of the cave, and one could not even see out to where the ice began again.

"Let us try to go over the land, to the North,"

Ivalu said. "I know the way to Netzilik, and we can reach it by tonight. There are people there, and we can eat and stay with them until the ice is strong again."

"It looks as though I am a man for whom a woman must decide," Bozi said. But he smiled and was happy, and they decided to do as she said.

It was not possible to take the sled with them over the mountain, as they would have to climb and crawl. They were two people who were trying to save themselves, and each had only a few skins rolled together. They put these on their backs, and started. Ivalu walked ahead, calling the dogs, and Bozi followed behind with the whip, to drive them forward.

It was very cold·up on the mountain but they had the wind in back of them and kept moving. From time to time he asked her whether she was freezing, but she always said no, that she was warm enough. She said that when they came to Netzilik she would find a woman she knew who had many skins. "She will give me her new boots, which she sews very well."

"But do you think she will do it? We have nothing with which to pay her, and perhaps she needs them herself."

"I will tell her that she must. I am your wife and I must be dressed well. In our land a man feels shame when a married woman shows by her clothes that he, her husband, has been behind in his catching. It is different for unmarried women. They should go badly dressed, in order to show how important it is to have a husband."

"In my country it is often different," Bozi told her. "Men give little thought to their women's passion for fine clothes."

She laughed at his words, and went on, often saying to herself, "Kar-el Boe-zeen—Karel Boezeen—" She wanted to be a woman who carried the right name of her husband in her mouth when they arrived. "I will have to call you when others can hear me. They will wonder and laugh and think great thoughts about me—"

They had a long road ahead of them. By the time darkness came they could see the mountains on the other side of the glacier. From this they knew they had reached the top, and that they did not have to climb any higher. Now they would be able to go forward more quickly. But once Ivalu stopped and seemed to be thinking. "Are you sure that this is the right way?" Bozi asked, worried.

"He who has been here once before does not forget it again," Ivalu told him. "But I am thinking of the way that lies behind the hills in the fjords."

"How far is it to there?"

"That we will see when we know whether the snow is lying high on the lee side."

They talked this way to one another, and then Ivalu said, "No one can tell the length of a road if he does not know fast the one is who is asking." Bozi wanted to show her he knew more than she and told her that the road is always the same length, whether one walks or rides with fast dogs. She laughed at this and did not want to speak of it any more.

When they reached solid ground they rested. "One is a little burdened by the unaccustomed boots," she said.

"Poor little Ivalu, I feel sorry for your difficulties," Bozi said, and wanted to rub her feet with his hand. But she only laughed and said there was no life without difficulty. "One must never feel sorry for anybody. That brings only greater pain to the one you feel sorry for. When one laughs at difficulties, they are easier to bear."

They went on again and Bozi thought of what she had said. "You are wiser than I," he said, "although I thought I was the wiser." At this she laughed again.

Now they were going down hill and Bozi wanted to take her hand. "No," she said. "I am neither tired nor in danger, and keeping in step is more tiring."

When they reached the ice below them she said it was strange that one could not see the houses.

"Are you sure these are the right fjords?" he asked again—but she did not answer, and went on.

After they had gone a little farther the dogs picked

up the scent, lifted their heads, and went into a gallop. They smelled the houses.

"The dogs in the settlement do not howl," Ivalu said, "and there are no lights in the windows. Perhaps the men are out for catch. Yes, surely, they are out on the new ice, and the women are asleep. Our coming will awaken them."

She said this but she doubted her own words. She knew right away that the settlement was deserted. She had wanted to come here and be a woman with a husband, and be envied when she had told them all about him. But now she was worried that Bozi would be impatient and angry. Maybe he would say that it would be better to be without a wife than to have one who failed him already on their first trip.

With these thoughts in her mind they reached the houses, which were lying in darkness. But just then the moon came up and they saw that everything was covered with snow and that there were no people. There was not even a dog, and no tracks of people or dogs, except those of their own and of a few foxes.

They remained standing in silence for a while, and she thought, "Yes, now he is angry, and he will speak harsh words. It will be like the feel of a wound to have him say the things he will say."

Ivalu was scared. She almost cried, then she thought of showing him a face which would not give away her thoughts.

"I am sorry for you," she heard him say. "Poor little Ivalu—you are a woman with a man who cannot help you. At first we had to lie in a cave where it was cold. Then you had to walk over glaciers—and now I have brought you to a deserted settlement and can't even give you anything to eat. Are you angry, Ivalu?"

She became a different woman, through his words. He had said them without anger or hardness. She looked up at him with a wonderful feeling, and then she let her thoughts go. Folding her arms around him she pressed herself close to him. Never, never did she think that a man could be so good and know so well what she would like to hear more than anything else in the world.

"Karel Boezeen," was all she said.

He did not quite understand what she felt. He was only happy that there was no disappointment in her over all the things which had happened to them in the last few days.

Chapter Nineteen

THE house into which they came was cold, but it was better than the cave. Ivalu had brought two lamps with her, to give as presents to the women of the place, and now they found them very helpful. There were sealskins on the plank beds and much dried grass underneath, so that their bed was comfortable. The few skins which they had with them, however, made only a poor cover.

They found no food, either in the house or on the meat scaffold, and they unharnessed the dogs so that the animals would not eat the harness or the ropes. Then they went into the house, closing the entrance behind them.

The dogs had found some remnants of food which had been thrown away, and were eating them. At least they would not starve. The two people did not yet feel hunger: they looked at each other and wanted nothing else. They went to sleep and woke up happy —bad luck had overtaken them, but they would not let it conquer them.

In the morning Bozi went out. He took his gun and wandered high up in the mountains, but he did not find even a hare. He saw the tracks of some and heard snow chickens nearby, but, when he got to them, a fox was chasing them. He followed for a long time, but he saw neither the fox nor the birds again, and he was very tired and without prey when he came home in the evening. By that time it was so dark he could not even see his gun barrel.

On his way to the house he thought of Ivalu, and of what she would say when he returned with empty hands. He felt it would hurt him if she was disappointed. But he had tried very hard, running all over the countryside while she rested.

The dogs howled as he came toward the house and he saw Ivalu coming out to meet him.

"It is nice that you have come home. I have sewn new shafts for your boots and kept busy all day long. Now that you are home I am happy and have no other desire."

Not a word did she say about his hunting, or ask whether it had been successful. So he told her about it, himself, and she said it was good to be without food for a while, for then one enjoys it so much more when again there is some in the house.

When they went inside he saw that she had cleaned the house of snow and gathered up all the remnants of old blubber. She had looked under the planks in all the houses and found a good deal of it. And a cooking lamp was burning—not a real one, but one which Ivalu had made out of an old rusty tin which had been thrown away. Yes, she had done a great deal, and in her work she had been luckier than he. His praise made her eyes big and her smile wide.

They forgot their hunger again and slept so deeply that their stomachs could not wake them—then the new day came.

On the day before Bozi had seen, from the top of the mountain, that the storm had broken up the ice outside these fjords, too. In the fjords themselves the ice was quite safe, but further out the water was black. This meant that it was impossible for them to go further north. So he took his gun and went out again.

"Are you going out for catch?" Ivalu asked, and this was her parting remark.

He took the same road as on the day before, but he saw no more hares. He looked in the valleys and he climbed the hills. There were fresh tracks, and traces of them, but the hares themselves were gone. He heard a fox barking in the mountain and went up there, but he saw nothing. After a while he became discouraged and sat down. He was here in the north, where he wanted to be, but he did not want to die of starvation. He wanted to live and make the people better. This thought gave him new strength to continue—so the day passed. When he could no longer see, he was forced to return home.

"I have made your boots smaller and now they will fit," Ivalu said. She had cut the soles smaller and then sewn the boots together again. She had been careful to make no light until it was necessary, she said. But he could see that she was saving the blubber for him.

Hunger was strong in him but he saw she was happy and he did not want to say anything. A man must be the last to show weakness when two are together, he said to himself.

Ivalu had killed a dog and cooked a pot full of meat. "That will give warmth to our bodies," she said. "Perhaps tomorrow we can continue on our journey. There is a small sled here, one with which the children must have played, which we can use for our trip. And it is better, anyway, not to have too many dogs pulling it." This was what she said, but she did not want him to understand that she doubted his ability to get meat.

When he went to bed he was still thinking of meat. When a man has no food for his wife he thinks a great deal, and his own hunger was strong, for a white man is not broken in to hunger from childhood.

"I will try again," he said the next morning as he went out, but it happened the same way. By now hunger had made him weak. He decided to go to the edge of the ice and keep a lookout for seals. He saw them come up in the distance, but he was helpless without a harpoon. He got closer, and one seal came up, turned around, and glared at him for a long time. Its big eyes were round and questioning, and he was teased into sending a bullet into the animal's forehead. The seal fell backwards into the water, and was instantly killed—but it drifted away and could not

be reached. At first he thought of jumping into the
water, for like most white men he could swim. But
it was too cold and might have cost him his life, so
he let the seal drift away and decided to try again to
find something on land. It was evening and there was
a moon which gave him light enough to shoot by.

He walked and walked. He would not return home
until he had something to take with him. But the
evening passed and still he had found nothing. He
thought of Ivalu at home waiting for him, and he
thought of her worrying and crying with fear.

When Ivalu heard his steps she came out and wel-
comed him. She asked no questions and her eyes
showed no worry because there was nothing to eat.
She only laughed, and again told him how she had
worked all day. When they went into the house, she
told him that she had had the idea to tear down the
meat scaffold of the settlement, and, after doing this,
she had found two seal fins which had fallen between
the stones. "I was a little hungry, and you stayed
away so long that I ate mine. But here is yours. I
cooked it before you came back, and I had to cook it
slowly so as not to use too much blubber."

Bozi took his seal fin. There was no thanks in his
words, but there was thanks in his greedy eating.
Only after he had eaten did he notice that he was
exhausted from having been without food for three
days. The fin tasted as good to him as food tastes to

one in childhood. He chewed off the skin, which had
been softened by the long cooking, and between the
bones was wonderful fat meat. He even crunched the
bones in his teeth, and, when he was finished, he
began to say words of thanks to his wife.

"But why did you eat yours before I returned?
Were you so very hungry?" he asked, after he had
swallowed the last bite of his. "Where are the bones
of your fin?"

"One threw them to the dogs in the house passage."

Instantly he knew she was lying.

"You are lying to me," he said, angrily. "You
spoke without truth. You did not find two seal fins—
you found only one and you gave it to me!"

"You went out every day and you looked much
more tired than I. If you keep up your strength, you
can bring home catch, but, if you weaken, it is the
end of us both. Seal fins do not taste good to me,
anyway."

Now he felt shame in his body because he had
eaten everything before thinking of her. His thoughts
were weakened by hunger, so that he felt pity only
for himself—and of Ivalu he did not think. It was
as if he had been asleep, but now his awakening was
a sickness. For even when men feel shame because
they have been made ridiculous, it is still not as bad

as finding out for the first time that they are unworthy.

"What can I tell you, my wife," he said. "Something happened that makes me sad. I forgot that we were two, and that it was I who was to get food for both of us. Now my wife has fed me! Ak yes! what a great catcher I am. What protection for my wife!"

Ivalu laughed at him and said she could not understand his talk. "But anyway, let us go to bed now. As long as we both live we will soon be able to get food for ourselves. Tomorrow we shall kill a dog, and from that food we can live until the ice gets strong enough for us to return home to our many possessions."

Then she was silent and looked at him wonderingly, to see if he would say anything. "Our many possessions!—what was it I just said?"

"Yes," Bozi said, "everything that was only mine now belongs to both of us. But now I must go out. I am filled with humiliating thoughts and I shall try to shoot in the moonlight. Let the food, which you gave me, strengthen me until something comes my way."

A man who wishes to go must never be stopped by a woman. So Ivalu said only that she would put fresh grass in his boots, as she had dried some over the lamp.

She was again alone and now she was a little afraid

that he was angry. But he, too, was alone—and he, too, was a little afraid. Perhaps he would be unable to get food for his wife, then she might be sorry that she had not eaten before. He walked quickly through the valley and this time his way led to the right place.

There was a hare jumping around in the moonlight, and there were several other hares with him. Bozi's shot cracked the silence and the first hare lay dead. He could not get near the others and it was some time before he could kill a second one.

The moon had travelled only a very little before he returned home with his prey, and his face showed his happiness. Ivalu ran out to meet him when the dogs howled. Maybe he was coming back with anger and resentment, she thought. Maybe she had better remain seated in the house, as other women do—but she was restless and went out.

"Ak! a great catcher lives in the place where I am! I was afraid that, when I awoke, my dream would be laughable. Did you really shoot? But that is impossible by moonlight! Ak! but I see you have killed two!"

Ivalu was so happy she said big words. She was happier over the hares than women in other places would be if they were told that a narwhal or a bear had been caught. For the two hares now meant "You can stop having hunger gnaw at you!"

Ak! she became so happy that she wanted to put her arms around Bozi again, and say nice words to him—and she did. He was quiet, and took her head in his hands. They were people with happiness in every part of their bodies, who were now going into the house to eat.

They ate the warm intestines and the liver tasted like the longing for sun in the winter darkness. They cooked the meat of one rabbit, drank soup, and ate their fill. They slept without freezing, and the warmth given them by the cooked meat lasted until the next morning.

Ivalu had cleaned an old pot, and now she cooked the second hare, making more soup and meat. By today Bozi was sure of himself. He knew they were going to live through.

It started to get cold again. The frost sat on his chest and built ice waves in his beard. A cold wind came toward the land, and Bozi thought, "Tonight the sea will freeze, and seals which I shoot in the water will drift toward the shore, and will not get lost."

It was not long before he returned home dragging a seal over the ice. Then there was happiness for him and for Ivalu, fodder for the dogs, and blubber for the lamps. Ivalu had found some old pieces of tin out of which she had made lamps, and they had warmth in the evening and through the night. Now they could dry their boots and mittens and have them pleasantly warm for tomorrow's journey.

For on the next day they were off for home. The ice was now two days old and could carry them. Ivalu wore the peculiar boots which she had sewn out of the old sealskins she had found under the planks. She had put dried grass in them, and they were warm.

They rode over the glacier on the little sled. Most of the time they both could sit. Bozi only walked when they were going uphill—then he was a man helping his wife. When they got to the top of the mountain they left the sled, and climbed down the other side to their cave. There, for the first time, they had seen each other as they really were—this was the first place where they had been together. They felt as though it were their home, but they hoped that this time it would not have to shelter them as long as it had the last.

They found the sled they had left, and the meat, the cooking apparatus, and their whole camp. They slept warmly and well, and when they awoke in the morning their backs felt no tiredness. Bozi went out on the ice and saw that it was safe for their journey. Now he would be a man riding back to his settlement with his wife. He would be a man who lacked nothing, and at whom no one could laugh any more and call a "bachelor."

The ice was fast but in several places it was thin,

and there they had to go slowly. They stayed close to shore until they reached strong ice, for here the sled runners were almost cutting through

"Are you afraid?" Bozi asked.

"Has a woman fear when she is travelling with her husband, and he is looking out for her safety?"

He knew his question was hiding his own fear.

Strong ice after a dangerous ride is like food after hunger. They laughed at one another and Bozi cracked the whip over the dogs so that they started to gallop. The sled, gliding over the ice and snow with the familiar sound, sounded to them as though it were laughing, too.

They saw three sleds coming toward them. They were catchers from Umanak: Uvdluriak, returning from Cape York, and two others.

"Joy and happiness!" they shouted. "At last you are here again. One has missed you and become restless. But now our white man has returned and we shall have happiness again in our settlement!"

None of them saw Ivalu. She sat on the sled and behaved like a woman to whom one does not speak. Her experiences were meaningless, and could be told on some occasion to the women, when they would find it convenient to listen to her. It was a man who was arriving, and it was him whom they greeted. The load on his sled could not be counted as important as the man himself.

But Uvdluriak wanted to be friendly, for it was his step-daughter who sat there. He called to Bozi that his dogs must be tired. "Let me drive your load."

But Bozi said, "No—it is true these dogs are tired, but still they can pull the load." And then they rode on.

Four sleds were driving homeward now. The dogs were eager and galloping, and soon they arrived. The moon shone, it was light, and many people had run to Bozi's house when they saw the sleds turn in that direction. The women were standing in a row outside, but Ivalu went straight in. Her boots were a wonder, and there was whispering and talking among the sewing women of the settlement.

"Did you see her boots? One has lost the foot-dress on the journey. Did they have a fight and lose their clothes? Then that must have happened while she was undressed!" And they giggled and laughed but no one really knew anything.

The women whose husbands had gone out looking for Bozi hurried to their sleds to help tie the dogs and to find out what had happened. But the men had heard nothing, and so were reserved and said that women's talk belonged to the bed planks, before the trappers themselves came home.

Shortly afterwards they all went in to visit those who had returned—and there they could really see Ivalu's clothes. Her pants would become a legend,

and her boots were even worse than they could see
outside in the darkness! There must be a lot to be
told, and Bozi, who came back with the woman
Minik had carried off, must also have something to
say.

But all that was said was said to Elias, and then
only the words that were necessary to have him make
tea. They ate, and talked about the journey the three
of them had made to the south. They laughed about
the big iceberg that had burst from anger over the
blood of the bear. They thought, laughing, of how
hungry they had been when they reached Mayark's,
and of the enormous amount of food they had eaten
there. They would remember that for a long time to
come.

But the women talked among themselves about
the little woman, who had come home with the white
man. She had always shown a peculiar mind, and was
so different from the rest of them. One could never
know whether one liked her or not. She was Ivalu.
They whispered and chattered among themselves
until Kazaluk became a little angry.

"Do not talk about my daughter," she said. "Is
she not just a woman who must adjust herself to
men? Are men so much after your own daughters
that they fight deadly battles over them?"

Her words had hit the two sitting next to her. For
the daughter of one was very bad in sewing, and an

old trapper who had become a widower actually had to be asked to take her. The daughter of the other had so little hair on her head that it could not be tied on the top. The people laughed at that couple and once someone put a bunch of musk-ox hair on the doorstep of the husband. So the two women were quiet when Kazaluk spoke. Now she continued:

"It is a misfortune to be so desired, for the man who lost out, destroyed her possessions out of revenge. Ak! I mourn for my little daughter!"

Then she went to Ivalu and they both went into another room. Ivalu walked very freely and without modesty, and Kazaluk saw that many of them were looking at her.

"Some clothing has been spoiled on the journey," Ivalu said. "It would not be unpleasant if other things were sent in their place." Then she was quiet and her mother said nothing. There would be shame in the family if the following day should pass without other pants being sent, or if these same boots should still be seen on her legs.

"Should you not have gotten off the sled and gone into our house?" Kazaluk asked.

Ivalu's answer would be very important.

"One finds these words strange," was all Ivalu said.

She went out again to the others, with no shame

because of her clothes, and without running home to get new ones. The women did not know what was going to happen next. Ak! the foolish Ivalu! She was always like a man in her decisions. Even when her real marriage partner had died, she had said impudent words against his relatives! Young and old were often angered because men admired her so much, and now here she was, sitting near the white man and behaving like the woman of the house. Maybe she would even go so far as to tell them to eat and drink—for she had taken food for herself as married women do in their own homes.

But the men were getting up to go, and the women had to do the same. Kazaluk looked at Ivalu, but her daughter looked at others, and did not go along home.

On their way the people began to talk aloud of Minik and Ivalu, but Kazaluk became angry again.

"Leave my little daughter free from the weight of your words," she said. "She happens to remain in the house of the white man. Perhaps he wishes to replace her clothes. Perhaps she does not wish to come with us because of her appearance. My daughter has the sorrow of being liked by many men. It is a burden, but often it leads to happiness in the end. For in beauty there is strength."

They all went to bed, and on the next day Kazaluk came with skins for Ivalu. Her daughter was not yet up, but was lying in Bozi's bed. She did not want to show herself in her ridiculous clothes again.

Pants and boots were sewn. And, after a few more nights' sleep in Bozi's house, Ivalu began to tell the women they should eat and drink when they were sitting at Bozi's table. She had some of the others bring skins for her, and one day she asked Samik's wife if she would chew a few birdskins. "I have too much to do with the fox skins Bozi has bought and cannot, therefore, chew the skins for his shirts. If you do them nicely, it is not impossible that I shall give you a few needles for it."

Samik's wife took the skins but ran quickly to the others to tell them that Ivalu was behaving like a man. She made others work and promised them needles in payment! But Kazaluk said that her daughter had good reason for her talk. As long as she lived in Bozi's house she had to look out for him until she moved away from there.

And then one day Ivalu visited her mother.

"One is lonesome for the little step-sisters," she said. She had brought good-tasting things in her cowl and gave them to all of them. "My mouth is a little tired from so much good taste," she said, and took out a platter of rotted walrus skin and liquid oil.

Quickly other women came, too. They said they wanted to visit Kazaluk while their men were out for catch. Like women, they chattered to one another

about their plans, some saying that now that spring
wanted to come they would soon move away.

"Perhaps we remain here," Kazaluk said, "and
perhaps we will journey to the north. I, miserable
woman, will wait here until he who decides has
spoken."

They spoke of other things, and then one took
courage and spoke directly to Ivalu. She was an older
woman, who was angered that Ivalu was sitting on
the bed plank with them, although she was young
and had no real husband who could have created respect for her by deeds of great catchings. She wanted
to mock Ivalu and asked her if any decisions had
been reached about her summer.

"Does a woman decide about her stay?" Ivalu
asked. "Can one who has a husband speak for herself? Ak! now old age has come to you and taken all
sense from your mouth!"

That was the big thing they had wanted to know.
A woman with a husband! Ivalu was married, to stay
with Bozi, and she said it without shame. Now they
could tell the strangest thing that the world had ever
seen. And one after the other the women left to go
home quickly and relate what they had heard.

Ivalu, herself, noticed that she had said what she
wanted to say without shame or fear of being laughed
at, and Kazaluk was smiling at her daughter. There
was understanding between them and Ivalu would

have liked to fall on her mother's neck and thank her for being different from the other women. For without her help, Ivalu could never have become Bozi's wife. But only to a white man could a woman show what she felt. Among the people she could only smile, for here women's thoughts were tied to their customs.

And so, when the men returned from catching, there was much talk in all the houses. Early the next morning sleds drove to the North and the South, each one wanting to be the first to tell the news: Bozi had now taken a woman for himself and was a married man among the people—and it was Ivalu, the daughter of Kazaluk and the granddaughter of old Merquzaq, whom the white man had married.

THE END